THE HAPPINESS COMPANION GUIDE

Glenn Ridless

First published by Dog Ear Publishing
4011 Vincennes Rd
Indianapolis, IN 46268
www.dogearpublishing.net

ISBN: 978-1-4575-5513-8

This book is printed on acid-free paper.

Printed in the United States of America

Preface

I know that my level of happiness is ultimately based on my everyday thoughts and actions. Happiness is a choice I make each and every day I spend in this wonderful experience called life. Life certainly has its ups and downs, how I handle the roller coaster ride is what inevitably determines my happiness. I am committed to living a proactive life. I also try to learn whatever I can from whatever extremely difficult lessons life throws my way. I have personally experimented with the fifty-two concepts in this book. I have witnessed the value of these thoughts by observing and conversing with people in my life's journey who have exuded a consistent lifelong happy attitude as well as with those who have not. I do not claim to be a totally, (100 percent), happy person. I do not believe anyone can be happy all of the time. Like most people, I am simply a human being trying to make the most out of my life, and I wish to experience the maximum amount of happiness.

I do not in any way claim to be profound. You might have already heard most of the notions that I mention in this book, but I may have a different way of presenting them. My ultimate goal is to help you help yourself transform into a happier person. After experimenting with the following ideas, I hope you will come to know and enjoy the happiness I have found. In my opinion, happiness involves sharing your wisdom with others; this is my purpose for writing this book.

Glenn Ridless

The amount of happiness
We experience
Is equal to the amount
Of permission
We allow ourselves
To have.

CHAPTERS

1.
GET YOUR PRIORITIES IN ORDER

We are busy beavers. We have activities, social events, careers, families, friends, and much more pulling us in many different directions. We try to live balanced lives in spite of our various responsibilities, but this is one area where we can really lose our sense of happiness. It is impossible to give equal time to everything in our lives; it is also unwise. Some things are simply more important than others, and it makes sense that we would want to spend more time in these areas. If we have not taken the time to sit down and define to ourselves how we should spend our time, then we definitely do not have our priorities in order. Imagine your life is graphed on a giant pie chart. There is only so much pie to go around, and there is only so much time to go around, as well.

First, you must decide what things in your life even deserve a piece of the pie. We spend a lot of our precious time on things that are neither necessary nor the least bit beneficial to us. Once we have removed what does not belong in our lives, we have to graph what does. Break down all the things going on in your life into major categories such as family, health, work, friends, and spirituality. Then decide how much time you want to dedicate to each area of your life.

Once you have done the planning, the only thing left is the doing. Spend your time in each area according to your chart's design. Even if you do not always succeed, you will be much happier knowing that you have attempted to plan your life instead of allowing it to plan you. Our time is our most precious commodity because it is so finite. Each of us gets a different amount of time to experience life; some of us use it wisely, and some of us don't. Life is not really all about how long we live; it's more about how much living we put into our lives.

We cannot control time.
We cannot make it go in reverse.
We cannot slow it.
We cannot prevent it from continuing.
We can only control what we do with it.

CHAPTER 1
AFFIRMATIONS

- I AM ORGANIZED AND IN CONTROL OF MY TIME.
- I DECIDE WHERE, WHEN, AND WITH WHOM I SPEND MY TIME.
- I PRIORITIZE THE CATEGORIES OF MY LIFE.
- I AM ABLE TO SAY NO TO A REQUEST OF MY TIME.
- I PLACE A GREAT VALUE ON HOW I USE MY TIME.
- I PLAN MY TIME & I STICK TO THE PLAN.
- I ALWAYS ARRIVE EARLY FOR APPOINTMENTS.
- I AM RESPECTFUL OF OTHER PEOPLE'S TIME.
- I USE MY TIME EFFECTIVELY.
- I GET THE MOST OUT OF EVERY MOMENT.

2.
THE PERSEVERANCE FACTOR

Webster's Dictionary defines perseverance as the ability to continue a course of action in spite of difficulty or opposition—that sounds like my definition of *living*! Some people believe that true happiness means having absolutely no problems, obstacles, or challenges in our lives. That sounds to me like a blissful death, but not a blissful life. Every step along the path of life has difficulties and challenges. If we do not maintain strong perseverance, our lives will become frustrating and unmanageable.

One essential for maintaining self-esteem is being confident that we can handle and cope with most obstacles we encounter. If we do not have strong perseverance, we will never accomplish anything; the minute a challenge arises, we simply quit. This will not get us very far in life and certainly will not make us very happy in the long run. Don't get me wrong, there are definitely proper times in our lives to give up on certain things or people, but only after very careful consideration and much perseverance.

To build strong perseverance, start with baby steps, by seeing small things through to the end. For example, you might finish reading a book, see a project around the house to completion, or solve a crossword puzzle. By building a series of small wins, you can move on to building a series of bigger wins, which will definitely make your life happier. You may start by being assertive with your overly demanding boss instead of quitting, seeking a marriage counselor instead of heading straight for divorce court, or sticking to a proper diet and exercise program to get back into shape. The list goes on and on … and so will you.

Life is simply one long journey.
The trail traverses
Through ease and difficulty.
The great lesson that life teaches us is
To enjoy and appreciate the easy times
And to learn and grow
From the difficult ones.

CHAPTER 2
AFFIRMATIONS

- I CAN OVERCOME ANY OBSTACLE.

- I KNOW AN UNLIMITED SUPPLY OF RESOURCES EXISTS.

- I AM CONVINCED THAT EVERY PROBLEM HAS A SOLUTION.

- I AM A CREATIVE PROBLEM SOLVER.

- I LOOK AT A PROBLEM FROM ALL ANGLES.

- I AM ABLE TO GO THE DISTANCE.

- I AM CONFIDENT THAT I WILL FIGURE THINGS OUT.

- I REALIZE THAT SOME SOLUTIONS COME IN THEIR OWN TIME.

- I ENJOY ASKING OTHERS FOR ADVICE AND RECEIVING CONSTRUCTIVE FEEDBACK.

- I KNOW THAT EVERY STRONG DESIRE CAN BE OBTAINED.

3.
THICK SKIN

One of the factors contributing to unhappiness is that we sometimes feel the people in our lives don't behave in the manner we think they should: People let us down. People aren't always considerate. People aren't always fair. People aren't always nice. People aren't always friendly. People don't always reciprocate our kindness. People aren't always in good moods. People aren't always thoughtful, generous, appreciative, or even polite toward one another.

Do I need to go on? I think you get the point.

The fact is, people aren't perfect, and they never will be. We should accept the fact that as we go through our lives, people may not—and often will not—live up to the expectations we have set for them. It is extremely rare, though not impossible, to meet someone who is either all good or all bad. For the most part, people are made up of good and bad, including their behaviors. That is part of human nature.

So, we can spend the rest of our lives feeling angry, hurt, jealous, upset, spiteful, vengeful, or depressed—or we can learn to overlook the occasional negatives and focus on the positives that people have to offer.

As free people, we have the right to associate or not associate with anyone we choose. We should take that right very seriously, especially when we realize we have allowed extremely negative people to infiltrate our lives.

When we are put into situations in which we must deal with people we would rather not, tolerance of others comes into play. We don't have to love or like everyone we meet, but we will experience greater happiness if we can learn to get along with one another as best as possible.

We cannot change people.
We can try to influence people.
We may not understand certain people.
We must try to tolerate all people
We don't have to like all people.
We should try to respect all people.
We can feel compassion for all people.
We must never accept abuse from people.

CHAPTER 3
AFFIRMATIONS

- I AM UNAFFECTED BY THE RUDENESS OF OTHERS.

- I AM NEGATIVITY-PROOF.

- I FOCUS ON BROADENING MY OWN LEVEL OF SELF-RESPECT.

- I AM ABLE TO DISCOVER THE GOOD IN EVERYONE.

- I ALLOW MYSELF TO FORGIVE OTHERS.

- I TAKE PEOPLE'S NEGATIVITY WITH A GRAIN OF SALT.

- I LET HARSH WORDS ROLL OFF MY BACK.

- I DO NOT LET THE BAD MOOD OF OTHERS AFFECT MY OWN.

- I JUDGE MYSELF BASED ON MY OWN STANDARDS.

- I CARRY NO EXPECTATIONS OF HOW OTHERS SHOULD BEHAVE.

4.
BE A GOOD PERSON

It may seem corny and outdated these days to want to be a good and decent human being. I think that's a real shame. What's wrong with wanting to strive to become a person of good character? The fact is that most happy people really are genuinely nice and kind. When you feel great about yourself and are enjoying your life experience, being a good person seems natural and effortless. Happy people seem to do the right thing when it comes to others: They are polite, considerate, sympathetic, helpful, kind, pleasant, caring, and concerned.

You will be surprised about how your attitude will change for the better when you simply desire to become a good person. Being a good person feels fantastic—especially when the inevitable positive reactions from the world start rolling in. What does it take to be a good person? Not much. The good news is that you don't have to be a perfect saint to be a good person. Just try putting yourself in someone else's shoes. Instead of rushing to judge or criticize someone, maybe lend that person a hand, or just sit and listen. There is no telling how far a single act of kindness will travel from one person to the next; if we all plant seeds of kindness, perhaps we can change the world for the better.

Most people in this world do not want others to solve their problems, but everyone needs to know, just once in a while, that somebody does care about them. A kind word, a warm smile, and a sincere thank-you may seem a bit old-fashioned nowadays, but these simple gestures are just as valuable as they have ever been. Remember, it's reciprocal: Goodness creates happiness, and happiness creates goodness.

It pays us back when we give it away.
Its smallest use can change a life.
Its greatest use can change the world.
It takes only a few moments to show.
It can last forever when it is received.
It is the simplest act that one can perform.
It has the most profound effect I've known.
It is the gift of kindness.

CHAPTER 4
AFFIRMATIONS

- I AM POLITE AND CONSIDERATE.

- I AM ABLE TO FEEL COMPASSION FOR EVERYONE.

- I ENJOY CARRYING OUT RANDOM ACTS OF KINDNESS.

- I AM WILLING TO LEND AN EAR.

- I LOVE TO HELP BUILD THE SELF-ESTEEM OF OTHERS.

- I LOVE TO COMPLIMENT PEOPLE.

- I AM GENEROUS I AM SUPPORTIVE AND ENCOURAG-ING.

- I SPEAK WITH KIND AND GENTLE WORDS.

- I AM A HELPFUL TEAM PLAYER.

- I AM A KIND AND CARING PERSON.

5.
DESIGN A FLIGHT PLAN

I am sure you have heard so much about goal setting that it may be coming out of your ears, but are you actually setting goals? Sometimes we don't do things because we don't see the value in them. Imagine an airplane taking off into the clear blue sky without a flight plan. It probably wouldn't get very far without colliding with another airplane and creating a major disaster. At the very least, it would eventually run out of gas and crash. If that airplane had took off during bad weather without a flight plan, its destruction would come even faster.

Are you getting the analogy here?

We need a sense of direction in order to be happy. We need a destination to have peace of mind. When obstacles and difficulties come our way—and they will come our way—our goals allow us to cope and to move forward.

Some people don't like to write down their goals because they feel trapped or pegged into a particular plan. Others don't like to write down their goals because they feel let down if they don't meet those goals. Goals shouldn't make you feel trapped, however; there is no rule that says you cannot change your goals whenever you feel it necessary.

If you don't reach your goal in a certain time frame, it is not the end of the world. Reset your goal, adjust it, or replace it all together. The point is that it is better to fly on an airplane with an amended flight plan than on one with *no* flight plan.

We all know that Murphy's Law can strike at any time. The more prepared we are to deal with life, the less the chance that we will permanently lose our sense of happiness. Designing a flight plan for ourselves allows us to be prepared. Knowing where we are headed in life is half the battle; getting there is the rest.

When we have determined our own destinies,
We can put up with the greatest of adversities.
When we have designed our own outcomes,
We can deal with any challenge that comes along.
When we know where we are headed,
We can outlast the negativity of others.
When we reach the finish line,
We will give tribute
To the vision that has carried us through.

CHAPTER 5
AFFIRMATIONS

- I FOLLOW A PLAN FOR THE WAY I WISH TO LIVE.

- I REVIEW MY LIFE'S VISION DAILY.

- I WRITE DOWN MY GOALS.

- I AM IN TOTAL CONTROL OF MY MIND.

- I TURN DESIRE INTO REALITY.

- I KNOW THAT WHAT I THINK RESULTS IN HOW I LIVE.

- I AM RESPONSIBLE FOR MY DESTINATION.

- I CAN ACCOMPLISH ANYTHING I CHOOSE.

- I DREAM BIG AND STRIVE HIGH.

- I IMAGINE MY DESIRED OUTCOMES.

6.
DISTINGUISH A JOB FROM A PASSION

We are not all fortunate enough to make a living doing something we are passionate about. Let's face it: We are often passionate only about putting food on the table and paying the light bill; we do what we have to do to survive. After all, life isn't always as glamorous as it seems in the movies. If we are working at jobs we are not passionate about, we need to admit that to ourselves. Sometimes we spend more time at work than we do at home. Doing an honest day's work for an honest day's wage is one thing, but pretending to love what you do is another. If we don't admit the truth, we may never attempt to create change, and perhaps we will never discover a way to make a living at something we feel passionate about.

When we do have passion for our work, we become happier. When we are passionate about our work, we are more productive and we become more successful, emotionally as well as monetarily. Usually when we are unhappy at work, it is because we realize we do not want to do it for the rest of our lives. By labeling this as a job instead of a passion, we can accept it and, as a result, take the time to plan for what we would really like to do. A boring or unfulfilling job can then become a tool to provide an income, instead of a lifelong sentence to misery.

Many of us hope to one day make a living by following our passion. Until that time, however, we can work at our present jobs, allowing us the time and income to pursue our dreams. As long as we are headed toward our passions, jobs we don't care for are simply a means to an end.

What is your passion? Can you make a living at it? Think about it and plan for it!

Passion sprouts from a strong desire
That is nurtured and cared for
Over a long time.
It grows and blossoms
Into an absolute obsession.
It then weaves its way around
Every obstacle it encounters,
Finally attaining its desired result.

CHAPTER 6
AFFIRMATIONS

- I KNOW WHAT THRILLS ME AND GETS MY BLOOD GOING.

- I AM PASSIONATE ABOUT MY LIFE'S VISION.

- I IGNORE ANYONE WHO TRIES TO STIFLE MY EXCITEMENT.

- I AM TOTALLY COMMITTED TO MY GOALS AND DESIRES.

- I AM ENERGIZED BY MY DESIRES.

- I AM A PATIENT PLANNER.

- I KNOW THAT FAILURE IS NOT AN OPTION FOR ME.

- I AM HONEST WITH MYSELF.

- I KNOW PASSION BREEDS MOMENTUM.

- I KNOW MY ENTHUSIASM IS A RESULT OF MY PASSION.

7.
DEFINE YOUR IDEA OF HAPPINESS

This book purposely gives various suggestions about how to live a happier life. It does not dictate or define individual happiness. Although I believe the ideas in this book will help enhance anyone's happiness, the responsibility of defining your own vision of happiness lies within you. Some of us have never taken the time to write down what our personal happiness would look, feel, and sound like.

We are often brought up to think that it is a virtue to deny our own happiness and to be concerned only with the happiness of others. I believe it is true that making others happy is a virtue; however, I also believe that denying our own happiness is a sin. We were given this wonderful chance at living for a reason, and it was certainly not to live miserable and unhappy lives, which would be a waste and misuse of our time here on Earth. A lot of splendor and magic went into the creation of our lives, and to deny our own happiness would be to insult our creation. We all make small sacrifices for the good of others throughout our lives because it bring us joy, but we need to allow ourselves to experience our own sense of happiness as well.

If you want happiness, you need to define what it means for you. Unfortunately, many of us often define our own happiness by accepting the definition from others. This can be a recipe for disaster. Living the ideals of others instead of defining your own can lead to always trying to please everyone but yourself. You may be able to fake your happiness to the rest of the world, but it is impossible to fool yourself. You owe it to yourself to define your own sense of happiness, and to appreciate and live out your own unique choices.

You alone design
The treasure map.
You alone determine
Where the treasure lies.
You alone decide
What the treasure is.

CHAPTER 7
AFFIRMATIONS

- I DEFINE MY IDEAL HAPPINESS.

- I HAVE A PERSONAL VISION FOR MY HAPPY LIFE.

- I AM ALLOWED TO DESIGN MY LIFE IN ANY WAY I WISH.

- I KNOW THAT HAPPINESS COMES FROM WITHIN.

- I AM ENTITLED TO AS MUCH HAPPINESS AS I CAN IMAGINE.

- I GENERATE MY OWN HAPPINESS.

- I KNOW THAT MY SENSE OF HAPPINESS IS CONTAGIOUS.

- I IGNORE THOSE WHO ARE NEGATIVE AND CYNICAL.

- I DESERVE TO BE HAPPY.

- I ENJOY SHARING MY HAPPINESS.

8.
ALWAYS REMAIN HOPEFUL

It is extremely difficult to maintain a happy life without hope. Hope is the belief that possibilities still remain. Hope lets us discover those little miracles in life that we otherwise couldn't come to know. If we lose all hope, we can no longer see the possibilities available to us, even though they are always there. If we believe that we are hopeless, we will give up our pursuit of happiness; restore a person's hope, and you will bring that person back from the dead.

Unfortunately, we do not always have the solutions for the problems we are struggling with, and we do not always achieve the things we are striving for when we think we should. Hope allows us to be optimistic that these solutions will arrive; we just need a little patience and a lot of perseverance. Hope confides in us that although we may not be able to understand everything that is happening to us at the moment, help is on the way. Hope allows us to keep positive mental attitudes, because it insists that life can always get better and that the best is still to come.

We all live with different levels and degrees of hope, and it takes a tremendous tragedy in life to lose it all. Remember, happiness never comes from just one thing. The surest way to lose all hope in life is to put all your happiness eggs in one basket. We hope for many things: We hope that we will make the right choices, that we will overcome the bad choices we have made, and that we will be able to enjoy life to the fullest. As long as we keep hope by our side, all forms of happiness are possible. Remember, hope fans the fuel for all our dreams and desires.

Hope makes all dreams possible.
Hope breeds perseverance.
Hope overcomes obstacles.
Hope removes fear.
Hope enables trust.
Hope creates new beginnings.

CHAPTER 8
AFFIRMATIONS

- I KNOW THAT EVERY CHALLENGE HAS A WAY OUT.

- I EMBRACE OPTIMISM AND A POSITIVE OUTLOOK.

- I KNOW THAT BETTER OPPORTUNITIES ARE ALWAYS LOOMING.

- I AM FOREVER AND UNRELENTINGLY HOPEFUL.

- I AM A POSSIBILITY THINKER.

- I CLING TO HOPE.

- I KNOW HOPE CREATES NEW BEGINNINGS.

- I KNOW THAT HOPE IS THE ANTIDOTE FOR DEPRESSION.

- I KNOW THAT AS LONG AS I HAVE BREATH, I HAVE HOPE.

- I GUARD MY HOPE LIKE A PRECIOUS GEMSTONE.

9.
FLEXIBILITY OF MIND

A closed and rigid mind will eventually become an obsolete mind. To survive, we need to maintain flexibility of thought as we encounter different circumstances. We are constantly evolving; we are not the same people now that we were as children. We have matured and changed our views as we have experienced the options that life has offered.

To live happy lives, we must continually be open to new ideas and new ways of doing things. The process of learning demands this of us. If you believed one idea to be true and then received information that proved it to be otherwise, what would you do? Would you continue believing the original idea because you were too set in your ways to change your mind? Unfortunately, that is exactly how a lot of people behave.

As we evolve as human beings, we constantly devise ways of making our lives more enjoyable not only for ourselves but also for those around us. A rigid and closed mind does not maximize an individual's sense of happiness, and it often contains outdated ways of thinking, such as prejudices, racisms, and superstitions that do not maximize the happiness level of others. It is one thing to hold a firm opinion on something you truly believe or to never give up on a particular goal; it is quite another thing to keep slamming your head into a brick wall, experiencing the same negative results because you are too stubborn to find a more efficient and successful way around the wall.

Decisiveness, firm character, and strong identity are characteristics of happy people, but flexibility and adaptability are the cornerstones of human survival. Without them, we would not have lasted nearly this long.

The mind is always rearranging ideas.
Always adapting to new information.
It distinguishes falsities,
And it clings to the truth.
If you listen to its wisdom,
The mind will always help you survive.
It will decipher the many codes in life
That you may encounter.
The mind is a tool that never stops working;
Only you can prevent it from doing its job.

CHAPTER 9
AFFIRMATIONS

- I AM ALWAYS OPEN TO NEW IDEAS.

- I LOVE TO DISCOVER NEW WAYS OF DOING THINGS.

- I VIEW EVERYTHING AS AN OPPORTUNITY TO LEARN.

- I EASILY ADAPT TO NEW SURROUNDINGS.

- I CHANGE MY BELIEFS BASED ON NEW EVIDENCE.

- I AM ABLE TO DO THE SAME THING IN MANY WAYS.

- I REALIZE THAT WE ALL APPROACH THINGS DIFFER-
ENTLY.

- I INCORPORATE OTHERS' HELP IN FINDING SOLU-
TIONS.

- I ENJOY THINKING OUTSIDE OF THE BOX.

- I AM ABLE TO REDIRECT MYSELF WHEN NEW INFOR-
MATION ARISES.

10.
CONTROL YOUR THOUGHTS

Most happy people will tell you that we are the sum of our thoughts, that we are what we think about most of the time. We can be as happy, young-spirited, and enthusiastic as we wish by preventing ourselves from thinking negative thoughts and by allowing only positive and productive thoughts to flourish in our minds.

This is not an easy task, however. It takes an enormous amount of discipline, desire, and practice to be in charge of your own mind.

Any thought that you repeat to over and over with strong emotional energy will eventually be accepted by your subconscious mind as the truth. The subconscious mind will then subtly direct your every thought and action to match what it believes to be reality. This system of the mind can be used to acquire the greatest heights of happiness or the lowest depths of despair. This is an automatic system. It does not judge right from wrong, good from evil, or happiness from despair; it merely does what it is told. Thus, we are the sum of our thoughts.

Some of lucky people in this world were raised in great, positive environments with nurturing, loving, and supportive parents guiding them and teaching them to have self-confidence and self-esteem, but a lot of us were not. The good news is that by using this natural system of the mind, absolutely anyone can proactively feed themselves positive and productive thoughts until those thoughts begin to take seed in the subconscious mind and come to fruition. We can experience any feeling we wish as long as we choose the input for our minds. In this way, we are no different than computers: Garbage in equals garbage out. We all have the ability to become the computer programmers of our own destinies.

What I strongly desire for myself,
I will eventually believe.
What I believe about myself,
I will eventually become.
If I desire happiness,
I will soon believe that I am happy
And will truly become happy!

CHAPTER 10
AFFIRMATIONS

- I AM THE MASTER OF MY THOUGHTS.

- I AM IN CONTROL OF WHAT I THINK ABOUT.

- I CHOOSE MY THOUGHTS AND WHAT I DWELL UPON.

- I USE AFFIRMATIONS TO HELP PROGRAM MY THOUGHTS.

- I DESIGN MY THOUGHTS TO CREATE DESIGNATED OUTCOMES.

- I AM THE SUMMATION OF MY REPETITIVE THOUGHTS.

- I THINK KIND AND LOVING THOUGHTS ABOUT MYSELF.

- I AM AWARE THAT THE MEDIA TRIES TO INFLUENCE MY THOUGHTS.

- I SURROUND MYSELF WITH POSITIVE THOUGHTS.

- I KNOW THAT MY ACTIONS FOLLOW MY THOUGHTS.

11.
BEWARE OF NEGATIVE PEOPLE

Negative people can cause great destruction to our own happiness. They are happiness saboteurs, their mission is to make you feel embarrassed, silly, immature, and stupid for having a positive and optimistic attitude toward life. Negative people come in all shapes and sizes, and in many disguises. They all have one common denominator, however, no matter how tricky they may be. If you have ever felt even the slightest bit worse about yourself after spending time with someone, you have experienced a negative person. Negative people like to make us feel as negative and as miserable as they feel. Some negative people try to bring us down on purpose, and some are not even aware that they are doing it; nevertheless, the result is the same.

Remember the system of the mind? Anything that is repeated over and over again with strong emotional energy will eventually become accepted by the subconscious mind as the truth. If it is true that we are the sum of our thoughts, then it is also true that we are the sum of the people we hang around with, because we will share their thoughts. The surest way to experience a lack of happiness is to choose to hang around a bunch of negative and miserable people all the time!

Sometimes we don't have a choice about who we hang around with at work or in our families. What can we do in such situations? Just being aware that negative people exist allows us to defuse their effect on us. We can recognize who they are, and if we are forced to deal with them, we can put up emotional force fields that will shield us from their negative bullets. Once you unmask negative people, you can see them for who they really are and deal with them accordingly.

In any great game, sport, or battle,
One must have a strong defense
To overcome a great offense.
We cannot possibly win
If we are unaware of how
We are being attacked.

CHAPTER 11
AFFIRMATIONS

- I AM NOT RESPONSIBLE FOR THE NEGATIVITY OF OTHERS.

- I SURROUND MYSELF WITH "CAN DO"-SPIRITED PEOPLE.

- I AM IMMUNE FROM THE EFFECTS OF NEGATIVE ENERGY.

- I REDIRECT THE SUBJECT WHEN THINGS TURN NEGATIVE.

- I TALK ABOUT OTHERS POSITIVELY.

- I SEE THE SILVER LINING IN EVERY OPPORTUNITY.

- I ENCOURAGE OTHERS TO BE GRATEFUL FOR THEIR BLESSINGS.

- I INSPIRE OTHERS TO CONCENTRATE ON SOLUTIONS.

- I OFFER A POSITIVE SPIN ON THE NEGATIVE MINDSETS OF OTHERS.

- I TEACH OTHERS TO FOCUS ON DESIRES INSTEAD OF FEARS.

12.
BECOME A TRUTH SEEKER

It is hard to feel happy if you are doing and saying things that you don't honestly believe in. Happy people seek out the truth in everything they do by trying to find the truths that apply to them personally. Living a life of genuine belief seems to put everything else in sync. When you find your inner truth, you can set your own standards and will always have the discipline to act upon what is in your best interest.

Sometimes, negative people say things to us, about us, that just aren't true. Unfortunately, these people can include those who are close to us, such as our parents, supervisors, or even spouses. They may say terrible things like "you aren't smart enough," "you're stupid," "you're lazy," "you will never amount to anything," or "you're ugly!" If we are not truth seekers, we may end up believing the lies these negative people have to offer. By accepting such lies as truth, we greatly damage our ability to lead happy and productive lives. Just because someone or some group declares that something is the truth doesn't necessarily make it so. You must become your own truth detective before you allow your subconscious mind to accept a belief. Your willpower is the only filter to your subconscious mind, so you must use it with great tenacity.

Remember, the subconscious mind does not know the difference between the truth and a lie, so if your filter fails to recognize a falsity and allows it to break through enough times, you will automatically accept it as the truth and start behaving accordingly! You will act lazy, believe you are stupid, and feel you are ugly even though none of these things are true. When you can totally believe and trust in all the choices you have made for yourself, you will experience a greater amount of happiness.

I will become my mind's gatekeeper.
I will decide what is right for me.
I will decide what is wrong for me.
I will determine what is true.
I will determine what is false.
I will make my own choices and decisions.
I will accept responsibility for my outcomes.

CHAPTER 12
AFFIRMATIONS

- I DECIDE MY OWN TRUTH.

- I AM ABLE TO DISCERN BETWEEN A LIE AND THE TRUTH.

- I AM A TRUTH DETECTIVE.

- I INVESTIGATE THINGS BEFORE I ACCEPT THEM FOR TRUTH.

- I CONSIDER THE MOTIVES BEHIND OTHERS' WORDS.

- I CREATE MY OWN OPINION ABOUT MYSELF.

- I DETERMINE MY SELF-WORTH.

- I LIVE LIFE ON MY OWN TERMS.

- I KNOW THE TRUTH MAY BE AFFECTED BY DIFFERENT POINTS OF VIEW.

- I ALLOW OTHERS TO EXPRESS THEIR PERSONAL TRUTHS.

13.
MAINTAIN A "CAN DO!" SPIRIT

Happy people are optimistic and believe they can accomplish whatever they set their minds on. They have the self-confidence to design plans and see them through to fruition. They are also extremely confident in their abilities to overcome any obstacles that may come their way.

Having a "can do!" spirit does not mean thinking you already know how to do everything. It *does* mean that you are able to figure out how to do most things based on the proper use of your resources. For example, if you have a great idea but not have the knowledge or skill to make it happen, you can still see your idea flourish by seeking out the aid of the people who may possess this skill or knowledge and recruiting them to become part of your endeavor. The mantra for the "can do!" spirit is "where there is a will, there is a way!"

Sometimes we feel that we live in a world filled with a "can't do" spirit, a world filled with pessimists and expert doom-and-gloom predictors. These types of people are destined to lives of mediocrity because they will always sit on the sidelines of life, critiquing everyone else instead of taking some risks and joining in the game.

Nothing worth accomplishing is without some amount of difficulty. If it was, then everyone would do it! Happy people find a way to rise above their adversities, managing to block out all the "can't do!" spirits and seeking out all the "can do!" spirits until they have accomplished whatever they have set out to do.

Along the way to any goal, we may get frustrated, angry, upset, depressed, impatient, scared, anxious, or disappointed, but with a deep-seated "can do!" spirit, we will always prevail. That's what happy people do: They make things happen!

"What will you be? What will you be?"
Said Aunt Naysayer to young Freeman Mcfree.
"A doctor? A lawyer? An engineer?
A writer? An actor? A business career?"
Said Freeman Mcfree as bold as could be,
"I want to be a lion!"
Aunt Naysayer looked at him with a frown.
"You can't be a lion. Now quit clowning around!"
But Freeman Mcfree said, as bold as could be,
"I want to be a lion!"
Now, Aunt Naysayer was calm most of the time,
But enough was enough!
"Now, Freeman, come on!
You can't be a lion, for you'll be a man,"
But that didn't spoil any of young Freeman's plans,
Then Freeman Mcfree let out one mighty roar,
And he swallowed his aunt whole
With his great lion jaws.
Said Freeman Mcfree, as bold as could be,
"I am a lion!"

CHAPTER 13
AFFIRMATIONS

- I ACCOMPLISH WHATEVER I SET OUT TO DO.

- I KNOW THAT EVERY PROBLEM HAS A SOLUTION.

- I GET THE JOB DONE!

- I FIND A WAY AROUND EVERY OBSTACLE.

- I AM A CHANGE MAKER.

- I CREATE A POSITIVE EFFECT ON MY ENVIRONMENT.

- I DO WHATEVER IT TAKES TO FINISH WHAT I'VE STARTED.

- I MAKE THINGS HAPPEN.

- I MAKE USE OF ALL THE RESOURCES AVAILABLE TO ME.

- I AM ABLE TO TRANSFORM MY VISIONS INTO REALITY.

14.
WHAT IS YOUR ULTIMATE PURPOSE?

There is a difference between goals and an ultimate purpose. Goals are the individual field markers for the things we wish to accomplish. They may be physical, spiritual, financial, or something else. An ultimate purpose can best be described as the main thing in life that makes you jump out of bed in the morning and allows you to greet the day with an optimistic and positive "can do!" spirit. An ultimate purpose is your number-one desire, your main priority, and your overall fuel for energy and enthusiasm. It is your essence! If you have an ultimate purpose, you will experience greater joy in life than if you don't have such a purpose.

Instead of living life by completing a series of unrelated goals, you can tie all your goals together to work toward your one ultimate purpose. This brings a tremendous amount of harmony, simplicity, organization, and synergy into your life. By the way, harmony, simplicity, organization, and synergy are also great symptoms of happiness.

Most people agree that an ultimate purpose would bring greater happiness to their lives, but the problem lies in the fact that they can't figure out what their ultimate purpose should be. You are the only person who can decide what your ultimate purpose should be. If you don't know what it is just yet, don't sweat it! Just keep repeating to yourself, "I desire to discover my ultimate purpose." I promise you that it will eventually come to you, probably when you least expect it. (If you keep repeating to yourself, "I don't know my ultimate purpose," you will program your subconscious mind to never know what your ultimate purpose is, and you will never discover it!

We are the architects of our own happiness. We can design lives that give us great meaning as well as great pleasure, and when we direct our lives towards an ultimate purpose, we can experience joys beyond our wildest imaginations.

It defines my every action.
It surrounds my every thought.
It negotiates all my choices.
It fuels all my enthusiasm.
It ignites my imagination.
It promotes all my ideas.
It drives all my passion.
It creates all my energy.
It is my ultimate purpose!

CHAPTER 14
AFFIRMATIONS

- I HAVE UNCOVERED MY ULTIMATE PURPOSE.

- I CREATE SYNERGY IN MY LIFE WITH MY ULTIMATE PURPOSE.

- I KNOW WHERE I AM HEADED AND WHAT I DESIRE.

- I AM PASSIONATE ABOUT MY ULTIMATE PURPOSE.

- I AM FULL OF ENERGY AND ENTHUSIASM.

- I KNOW THAT MY ULTIMATE PURPOSE BENEFITS MANY PEOPLE.

- I AM FULFILLING ALL MY DREAMS AND DESIRES.

- I TAKE MANY SMALL STEPS TOWARD ONE LARGE DESIRE.

- I ALLOW OTHERS TO TAKE PART IN MY ULTIMATE PURPOSE.

- I RELENTLESSLY PURSUE MY ULTIMATE PURPOSE.

15.
CONSTANT IMPROVEMENT

Ironically, happy people are never completely satisfied with themselves. We are often taught that true happiness leads to a spiritual state of awareness in which everything is perfect and harmonious. Reality, however, suggests that true happiness has a natural ebb and flow to it; without difficulties and challenges, we could never experience satisfaction and joy. A big part of happiness comes from setting and meeting various goals throughout our lives. The journey toward each goal gives us just as much exuberance as the goal's completion.

Happy people constantly strive to raise the bar, increasing their ability to learn more, love more, and live more. The beautiful thing about self-improvement is that it contains infinite possibilities. Have you ever met anyone one who was totally perfect? There is always room for improvement in all facets of our lives. That means that there should never be a reason for us to become too complacent with our lives; complacency leads to boredom. We don't have to focus on trying to keep up with the Joneses (as the saying goes), because that will not improve our lives.

There is plenty for us to take action on right in our own backyards. For example, we can improve upon our physical health and appearance, our financial status, our expertise levels, our wisdom, our sense of spirituality, our relationships, and our level of compassion for one another. You get the idea; this is a never-ending list.

I compare life to the game of golf: an individual sport in which you still compete against others. You focus on improving upon your own strengths and weaknesses, and then you play the game.

If we all spent time improving ourselves, we wouldn't have time to become critical of others. Happiness is in the striving!

Each step I take leads to another level.
Each goal I achieve inspires me
toward more challenges.
I do not rest upon what I have already done;
I strive to accomplish what I haven't yet.

CHAPTER 15
AFFIRMATIONS

- I UNCEASINGLY CONTINUE TO GROW, LEARN, AND IMPROVE.

- I KNOW THAT CONSTANT IMPROVEMENT BREEDS VITALITY.

- I DO MY VERY BEST, BUT I CAN ALWAYS GET BETTER.

- I SEEK ADVICE ON HOW TO IMPROVE MYSELF.

- I ENJOY THE SELF-DISCIPLINE REQUIRED TO IMPROVE.

- I BUILD WILLPOWER WHEN I SEEK TO IMPROVE MYSELF.

- I ENGAGE IN CREATIVE IMPROVEMENT.

- I EXCEL UPON MY EXCELLENCE.

- I COMPETE WITH MYSELF AND WITH MY LAST PERFORMANCE.

- I LOVE TAKING THINGS TO A HIGHER LEVEL.

16.
SEEK WORTHY APPROVAL

We all seek the approval of others. When we don't get it, the result is often unhappiness. When seeking the approval of others, we must keep things in perspective. Are they worth seeking approval from? Are they manipulating or using us in any way as a condition of giving their approval? Are they even in the correct mental state to be able to give us their approval? Do they have the proper expertise to make their approval valid? Are they emotionally, physically, or sexually abusive in return for their approval?

Many lives have been completely destroyed by when the approval of unworthy people has been sought. We have been brought up to believe that the authority figures in our lives should be good, kind, and wise people who are able to lead us to greater heights of self-esteem. Unfortunately, however, this is sometimes not the case. Parents, teachers, bosses, spiritual leaders, and coaches may not always be up to par; that is when we should stop seeking their approval. They are worthy only because of their actions, not because of their status!

It is, however, very rewarding and beneficial to seek out positive role models whose approval is worth seeking, people who will give the proper constructive criticism that you will need in order to continue to improve and reach your ultimate purpose in life.

We all seek acceptance and approval. Just remember to be very discerning and particular about whom you seek approval from—and don't forget that self-approval will bring you the most satisfaction! Happy people usually try to seek their own approval first. After all, is there anything wrong with becoming your own best friend? You, above anyone else, should trust, understand, and accept yourself!

I found approval in my own voice,
Not in the voices of the crowd.
I found self-esteem in my own image,
Not in the images that the world offers.
I found harmony within my spirit,
Not by giving in to peer pressure.
I found that I am my own best friend,
Not the sidekick to other people's egos.

CHAPTER 16
AFFIRMATIONS

- I AM AN EXCELLENT AND DISCERNING JUDGE OF CHARACTER.

- I AM PARTICULAR ABOUT TO WHOM I LEND MY TRUST.

- I PLACE GREAT VALUE ON HAVING A STRONG POSITIVE ROLE MODEL.

- I INVESTIGATE OTHERS' REPUTATIONS BEFORE I SEEK THEIR COUNSEL.

- I TRUST MYSELF MORE THAN ANYONE ELSE.

- I AM INSPIRED BY ROLE MODELS WHO ARE LIVING OUT THEIR PASSION.

- I GATHER ACCURATE INFORMATION, AND THEN I GO WITH MY GUT INSTINCT.

- I AM AWARE THAT EVERYONE WEARS SOME FORM OF SOCIAL MASK.

- I AM AWARE THAT NOT EVERYONE'S INTENTIONS ARE ADMIRABLE.

- I ACCEPT THAT EVEN FICTIONAL CHARACTERS CAN BE ROLE MODELS.

17.

SHOW RESPECT TO EVERYONE

Happy people don't have time to waste on being disrespectful to others, because they are too busy enjoying being joyful. Being respectful to those around us allows us to sleep soundly on the pillows of clear conscience. If we are consistently respectful to others, we can righteously hope that others will treat us the same way. If we think it is acceptable to be disrespectful to others yet expect respect in return, we are hypocrites and will create disharmonious consciences. A division in conscience always leads to unhappiness!

The most difficult people to be respectful of are the ones who do not reciprocate that respect, but it is imperative to our own sense of happiness that we do not stoop to their level. We must always take the higher road; in the long run, it is the only road that leads to a sense of inner peace and self-confidence. A tit-for-tat reaction might be satisfying at the time, but it has tremendous repercussions later—we become just as guilty as the person by whom we felt slighted.

Respect for others builds self-respect. Disrespect for others creates low self-esteem.

We were all uniquely created; therefore, every one of us is worthy of respect. We don't have to agree with everyone, understand everyone, or even like everyone, but we should always try to respect everyone. When we allow others the freedom to express themselves, we are also allowing ourselves the freedom to be unique. We can take great pride in becoming respectful. Pride builds self-esteem, and self-esteem is one of the key ingredients to a happier life.

Treat everyone like kings and queens,
And you'll be treated that way too.
Treat others like a doormat,
Then in return,
They will walk all over you!

CHAPTER 17
AFFIRMATIONS

- I KNOW WE ARE ALL CREATED EQUAL AND WORTHY OF RESPECT.

- I RESPECT EVEN THOSE WHO DON'T RECIPROCATE RESPECT.

- I GIVE EVERYONE RESPECT BECAUSE IT IS MY OWN PERSONAL VALUE.

- I KEEP MY EGO IN CHECK WHEN I GIVE OUT RESPECT.

- I TREAT EVERYONE AS BROTHERS AND SISTERS.

- I KNOW I MUST RESPECT MYSELF IN ORDER TO RESPECT OTHERS.

- I TREAT OTHERS THE WAY THEY WOULD LIKE TO BE TREATED.

- I DEMONSTRATE MY RESPECT WITH KINDNESS AND COMPASSION.

- I RECEIVE THE SAME PROPORTION OF RESPECT THAT I OFFER TO OTHERS.

- I RESPECT AND EMBRACE THE DIVERSITY THAT THE HUMAN RACE HAS TO OFFER.

18.
A GENUINE INTEREST IN OTHERS

When you are truly happy, you don't feel the need to brag about yourself or to try to impress others. Being comfortable with yourself allows you to take a genuine interest in others, which can bring happiness in many ways. Most people tend to like people who seem to be interested in knowing and understanding them. If people naturally like you, it will certainly bring you greater happiness in more ways than I can list here.

Taking an interest in others allows us to learn new things that we may not have had the chance to discover otherwise. People are interesting. They are like walking historical novels!

People love to share what they know and what they have experienced over the years. This wonderful free knowledge is at our fingertips. All we have to do is take a genuine interest in people, and they will be thrilled to share because we are willing to listen. When we have a genuine interest in others, they will have a genuine interest in us. The key here, of course, is the word *genuine*. Nobody likes a fake person who pretends to be interested just so they can gain favor in some way.

Being genuinely interested in others may open your world and put a fresh perspective on things. Our own thinking is always in danger of becoming redundant; sometimes we can get into mental ruts and can't think our way out. It is healthy to listen to people's viewpoints and thought processes. They may have greater years of experience or expertise on certain matters that may shed some light on our uncertainties. Their advice may become invaluable!

Taking a genuine interest in others allows you to become an outgoing and self-confident communicator, and a person comfortable in any crowd.

I can learn from others.
I can sympathize with others.
I can gain experience from others.
I can laugh with others.
I can acquire wisdom from others. I can exchange ideas
with others. I can receive advice from others.
I become fulfilled through others.

CHAPTER 18
AFFIRMATIONS

- I FIND OTHERS FASCINATING.

- I AM ABLE TO LEARN SOMETHING FROM EVERYONE.

- I GAIN SELF-UNDERSTANDING BY UNDERSTANDING OTHERS.

- I KNOW EACH PERSON OFFERS SOME FORM OF WISDOM.

- I ENJOY GETTING TO KNOW MANY DIFFERENT PEOPLE.

- I LOVE LEARNING ABOUT DIFFERENT CULTURES AND CUSTOMS.

- I LEARN FROM THE MISTAKES THAT OTHERS HAVE MADE.

- I FEEL ENERGIZED AFTER A GOOD CONVERSATION.

- I FIND COMMON GROUND WITH EVERYONE.

- I AM INTERESTING TO OTHERS BECAUSE I SHOW INTEREST IN THEM.

19.
PATIENCE

Patience can be defined as calm endurance, endurance of pain or trouble without complaint, or calm toleration of delay or confusion. We are no longer babies, so we don't have the luxury of receiving instant gratification. We can cry, kick, and scream all we want when things don't go our way, but it is highly unlikely that someone will come running to our aid; most likely, they will go running the other direction.

Patience is something we can develop. Happy people have developed patience to an optimum level. It is very feasible to get all we want out of life, but we don't always get it when, where, and how we expect. This is why we need an enormous amount of patience. Patience breeds the self-confidence that lets us know we can always complete what we have started, regardless of the obstacles or unforeseen circumstances that may come along.

If we develop patience within ourselves, we automatically have patience with everyone else. People work, think, speak, and perceive on all different levels; we must have the patience to relate with them at their levels if we are ever going to maintain happy and fruitful relationships.

Patience allows us to slow down and take the time to plan and organize our actions; it allows us to do things right the first time instead of rushing in all foolhardy and having to do it all over again.

Above all, patience breeds endurance. We all remember the story of the tortoise and the hare. Life isn't about how quickly you can get through it but is about the quality of the life that you lead. It takes patience to live a life of quality; we need patience not to settle out of fear that we'll never get the things we really desire.

Patience allows us
To reach the finish line
In spite of the many obstacles
That we may encounter.
Patience allows us
To relate with all people
By engaging them on
Their level of understanding.
Patience allows us
To be careful and cautious
And to count on doing
Things right the first time.
Patience allows us
The time to prepare
And to make the correct choices
To live lives of quality.

CHAPTER 19
AFFIRMATIONS

- I TAKE THE PROPER AMOUNT OF TIME TO DO THINGS CORRECTLY.

- I FINISH THE RACE NO MATTER HOW LONG IT TAKES.

- I KNOW THAT PATIENCE BREEDS COMFORT WITH THE SELF.

- I AM SURE AND STEADY.

- I ALLOW OTHERS TO SPEAK WITHOUT INTERRUPTING THEM.

- I AM A PATIENT PLANNER.

- I DEMONSTRATE PATIENCE TOWARD OTHERS.

- I AM A PATIENT LISTENER.

- I AM PATIENT IN OBTAINING MY DESIRES.

- I UNCOVER WISDOM WHILE I'M WAITING.

20.
REMOVE ALL FORMS OF ENVY

It is impossible to live happy lives when envy prevails in our thinking. This emotion can destroy dreams and dissolve relationships in the blink of an eye. Focusing on what everyone else has will in no way help you obtain what you desire.

Envy can very quickly create a crushing onslaught of low self-esteem. When we envy what other people own, do, or look like, we are relaying to our subconscious that those people are better than us and that we can never reach their heights of accomplishment, success, or happiness. Envy, which is extremely destructive, is so powerful that it keeps repeating its nasty message again and again until its victim is rendered utterly useless and helpless.

We can replace envy with admiration. We can pick positive role models whom we admire and can learn from them instead of hating everyone who seems happier than we are. We can learn a lot from others who have achieved the goals that we are after; envying them will only prevent us from seeking out their knowledge.

Some people may feel that envy is the motivating force in their lives. They may believe that this negative energy keeps them alert and on their toes, ready for the rigors of living. They may feel that becoming better than the next person will make everything all right. But if that's the case, when does it end? Whom do we have to beat next?

Negative motivators may work for a while, but in the end, they tear us down, leaving us tired and ineffective. Positive motivators, such as living life based on your own standards, not only create a happier life but also result in a vibrant abundance of energy.

It is like a monster
When it rears its ugly head.
It destroys relationships;
It crushes self-confidence;
It stomps on all our dreams.
It pretends to be our friend
While it whispers in our ears,
"They are better than you.
They are smarter than you.
They are more talented than you."
It is like a parasite.
When it plays on all our fears,
It soaks up all our energy;
It drains all our ambition;
It sucks up all our desires.
It is to be destroyed
Whenever it appears,
It is envy!

CHAPTER 20
AFFIRMATIONS

- I FOCUS ON MY OWN DESIRES.

- I ADMIRE EVERYONE'S ACCOMPLISHMENTS.

- I ENJOY CONGRATULATING PEOPLE.

- I LOVE TO CELEBRATE PEOPLE'S SUCCESSES.

- I LOVE TO SHARE IN THE HAPPINESS OF OTHERS.

- I SINCERELY COMPLIMENT PEOPLE EVERY DAY.

- I AM EXCITED FOR OTHERS WHEN THEY RECEIVE GOOD NEWS.

- I AM AN ENCOURAGING TEAM PLAYER.

- I MEASURE UP TO MY OWN STANDARDS.

- I GENUINELY DESIRE FOR EVERYONE AROUND ME TO FLOURISH.

21.
BE YOUR OWN BEST FRIEND

Who is the one person you can always rely on? If the answer is not yourself, then you probably have some work to do. You should always be your own best friend. Only after building a solid relationship with yourself can you offer healthy and constructive friendships to others.

One of the biggest human fears is the fear of being alone. Why are we afraid to spend time alone with the one person who should know us best of all? Most likely, it is because we have been programmed to avoid being alone; our parents always made sure that we were engaged in some activity that involved other people. After such conditioning, we grow up avoiding getting to know ourselves, and we seem to be able to discover who we are only through the eyes of people around us.

It is very dangerous to form our identities based only on how others view us. If other people are not decent and kind to us, we will grow up thinking there is something wrong with us, and we will develop lifelong feelings of inadequacy. We are born into this world alone, and we leave this world alone. Spending some time alone with ourselves should not seem out of the ordinary.

Time alone allows us to become acquainted with ourselves; it gives us time to decide upon our ultimate purpose and to set goals. It also allows us time to revitalize and rejuvenate our minds and bodies.

After spending time alone, I have learned that my own best friend (me) can be either kind or mean depending on how I have treated myself over the years. If you are deliberately and consistently putting good and positive thoughts about yourself into your subconscious mind, your own best friend will be a great ally; if you don't, you may end up becoming your own worst enemy.

I have stood alone many times,
Staring in the mirror.
Sometimes I saw my very best friend;
Sometimes I saw my own worst enemy.
I will continuously get to know myself
Until my reflection becomes an image
That I will always look forward to viewing.

CHAPTER 21
AFFIRMATIONS

- I ENJOY MY OWN COMPANY.

- I LOVE MYSELF UNCONDITIONALLY.

- I AM A NICE PERSON.

- I VALUE SPENDING TIME ALONE.

- I AM PROUD OF THE PERSON I HAVE BECOME.

- I ENJOY RELAXING AND RECHARGING.

- I AM MY OWN BEST FRIEND.

- I APPRECIATE A QUIET MOMENT TO MYSELF.

- I AM NEVER ALONE WHEN I'M WITH MYSELF.

- I HAVE LEARNED TO TRUST AND RELY UPON MYSELF.

22.
SPEAK KINDLY TO YOURSELF

We are all guilty of saying awful things to ourselves that we wouldn't dream of saying to anyone else because we would never want to hurt their feelings. What about our own feelings? If we are to be our own best friends, we need to stop all the bad-mouthing of ourselves and start encouraging ourselves instead. Here is a small example of some of the negative things we may say to ourselves regularly: I'm such an idiot; I am such a loser; I'm so fat; I'll never be good enough; I am not well liked; I am boring; I am ugly; I will always be broke. Though we wouldn't dare say any of these things to even the least of our friends, but we don't hesitate to say them to ourselves!

Remember once again that everything we repeat to ourselves with strong emotional conviction is accepted by our subconscious as truth. If you keep saying negative and unkind things about yourself, they will manifest, I guarantee. Now here is the great news: Everything is reversible! If you deliberately and consistently start saying positive and kind things about yourself, they will manifest, as well.

The world has enough negative saboteurs. You don't need to be one of them. From now on, try to catch yourself when you are saying negative things about yourself. Immediately rephrase what you were saying in a more encouraging manner. For example, if you catch yourself saying, "I am so dumb; I never get anything right," rephrase it as "I am new at this, but I am getting the hang of it." Eventually, this will become such an engrained habit that the subconscious mind will automatically do it for you and the negative self-talk will be permanently replaced by a positive and self-appreciative mind frame.

Happy people
Give the benefit of the doubt
To themselves.
Happy people
Don't talk badly
About themselves.
Happy people
Are always encouraging
To themselves.
Happy people
Focus on the good and kindness
That dwell inside of them.

CHAPTER 22
AFFIRMATIONS

- I TALK KINDLY TO AND ABOUT MYSELF.

- I GIVE MYSELF A PAT ON THE BACK.

- I REPLACE NEGATIVE SELF-TALK WITH POSITIVE WORDS.

- I GIVE MYSELF PEP TALKS.

- I ENCOURAGE MYSELF WHEN TIMES GET TOUGH.

- I SPEAK ENTHUSIASTICALLY TO MYSELF.

- I TALK TO MYSELF LIKE I DO TO A LOVED ONE.

- I HAVE COMPASSION FOR MYSELF.

- I KNOW THAT PERFECTION IS UNREALISTIC.

- I REPEAT POSITIVE AFFIRMATIONS EVERY DAY.

23.
STAY ENTHUSIASTIC

Enthusiasm is the positive energy produced through a purpose-driven, optimistic, "can do!" spirit. Enthusiasm keeps everything fresh, new, and exciting; it is the single greatest result of becoming self- motivated. Most of us start out enthusiastic about everything we do, but we don't always finish that way. Often, we start projects with full-throttle enthusiasm, and then, when obstacles creep in, we lose our enthusiasm, until we are no longer interested and quit.

We must remember that enthusiasm is always a result of a strong commitment to a goal, which then produces a deep-seated belief that the goal will be reached. To remain enthusiastic, we must pick goals that we really desire to achieve; otherwise, we will lose steam, because we can't stay enthusiastic about something we really didn't want in the first place.

We may not want to do everything, but we should be enthusiastic about the things we do. There is a price to pay for everything. It is imperative for us to realize that there are some things for which we are not willing to pay the price. Lack of enthusiasm is a sure sign. If we are not enthusiastic about the things we do, we need to double-check our true intentions, because we might be involved in something for the wrong reasons.

I define a cynic as someone who has lost all enthusiasm for living. Cynics' lives are dark and dreary, full of doom and gloom. If you are not careful when you are around cynics, they may suck all the enthusiasm out of you as well! Cynics want you to feel silly and immature for showing the least amount of enthusiasm toward anything. If we are committed to our goals, however, we won't allow cynical people to deplete our enthusiastic energy. This is why I say that we need to remain enthusiastic to live happier lives.

Enthusiasm is like liquid gold;
It is powerful and priceless.
When it runs through our veins,
It leads us and inspires us
To the greatest heights of happiness.
It creates an endless energy source
That gives us the stamina
To obtain our hearts' desires.

CHAPTER 23
AFFIRMATIONS

- I KNOW ENTHUSIASM FOLLOWS A STRONG CONVICTION.

- I APPLY MY ENTHUSIASM TO THE TASK AT HAND.

- I USE MY ENTHUSIASM TO PREVENT PROCRASTINATION.

- I AM ENERGETIC AND ENTHUSIASTIC.

- I AM ABLE TO HAVE CONTROL OVER MY ENTHUSIASM.

- I SHARE MY ENTHUSIASM WITH OTHERS.

- I HAVE A STRONG INTERNAL ENTHUSIASM.

- I KNOW ENTHUSIASM PROPELS ME TO PERSEVERE.

- I AM PROUD OF MY ENTHUSIASTIC ATTITUDE.

- I AM ENTHUSIASTIC ABOUT MY GOALS AND DESIRES.

24.
AN ATTITUDE OF THANKFULNESS

Happy people don't complain about every person who hurts their feelings, everything they don't have, or everything that didn't go their way. Happy people are thankful for all the wonderful, fantastic, and beautiful people, things, and situations in their lives. Happy people always try to maintain an attitude of thankfulness.

We are unhappy when we spend too much time focusing on what's wrong with our lives and very little time thinking about what is right with our lives. This does not mean that we should stop trying to improve ourselves; rather, it means that we can be happy and appreciative of who we are and what we have at the moment as we continue to strive and evolve.

No one is always happy. Happiness is a process; it takes work, planning, commitment, focus, and self-evaluation. We are all at different levels of happiness. Happiness is not based on only one thing or one idea; many things contribute to happiness. A lot more than the fifty-two suggestions in this book will lead to happier lives; this book is just the tip of the iceberg. You will discover the rest on your own journey through life.

If happiness is a process, do we have to be miserable along the way? No. An attitude of thankfulness creates patience and hopefulness, and it allows us to focus on the future, become appreciative of the present, and be grateful for the past. We are the sum of our experiences; whether they were positive or negative, they shaped us into who we are. If we are not who we wish to be at the moment, we can still be thankful that we have the ability to improve and to eventually become who we have envisioned ourselves to be.

I am thankful for my family.
I am thankful for my spouse.
I am thankful for my friends.
I am thankful for my house.
I am thankful for my wisdom.
I am thankful for my wealth.
I am thankful for my past.
I am thankful for my health.
I am thankful for my present.
I am thankful to be free.
I am thankful for my future.
I am thankful to be me.

CHAPTER 24
AFFIRMATIONS

- I AM THANKFUL FOR THE LESSONS THAT I HAVE LEARNED.

- I AM THANKFUL FOR THE LOVED ONES IN MY LIFE.

- I AM THANKFUL FOR THE THINGS I HAVE.

- I AM THANKFUL FOR MY COMPASSIONATE NATURE.

- I AM THANKFUL FOR MY ABILITY TO CREATE MY FUTURE.

- I AM THANKFUL FOR MY LOVING ATTITUDE TOWARD OTHERS.

- I AM THANKFUL TO BE ALIVE.

- I AM THANKFUL TO FOR MY ABILITY TO LEARN AND GROW.

- I AM THANKFUL FOR MY CREATIVITY.

- I AM THANKFUL FOR THE BEAUTY IN THIS WORLD.

25.
NONE OF OUR BUSINESS

Many people make themselves extremely unhappy by spending their time worrying about how everybody else is living instead of analyzing their own lives. Judging and criticizing the rest of the world is a defense mechanism that allows us to avoid dealing with our own challenges on the road to happiness. We are all entitled to our opinions, but true happiness involves accepting others. Prejudices and generalities about people or groups of people will build negative attitudes that will not only harm our own thinking but will also destroy the harmony in our relationships.

We don't have to like or believe in everything that other people do or say, but we should always remember that it is really none of our business. Isn't it enough to worry about our own lives? Don't we have enough things to keep us busy without nosing into other people's business? Show me a gossiper, and I'll show you someone who is extremely unhappy. Happy people simply do not have the spare time to critique everyone around them; happy people are doers.

Happy people are busy enjoying time with their families and friends, being creative and productive, and learning and improving; they take their precious lives very seriously and don't have time for nonsense—and gossip is nonsense. Are our lives so meaningless that we have to talk negatively about everyone else? Could it be that we gossip because nothing interesting is happening in our own lives? As long as people are not physically or emotionally harming others (including animals) or being destructive toward other people's property or the environment, we should conclude that what they do is none of our business. We should all appreciate the individual freedom that we possess; live and let live.

Concern yourself with positive things.
Do not waste time on foolish talk.
Raise yourself by building others up.
Focus on understanding and not on judging.
Help those in need;
Do not laugh at their misfortunes,
Focus on the good in others,
Allow others to choose their own paths.

CHAPTER 25
AFFIRMATIONS

- I PLAY IN MY OWN BACKYARD.

- I FOCUS ON THE GOOD AND POSITIVE IN OTHERS.

- I IMPROVE THE ENVIRONMENT AROUND ME.

- I APPRECIATE THE WEAKNESSES IN MYSELF AND OTHERS.

- I REMOVE MYSELF FROM A GOSSIPING FRENZY.

- I BUILD OTHERS UP.

- I UNDERSTAND OTHERS WITHOUT JUDGMENT.

- I LIVE A LIFE OF LOVE.

- I ENJOY HELPING AND ENCOURAGING OTHERS.

- I SPEAK WORDS OF PEACE AND KINDNESS.

26.
QUITTING TIME

Happy people have become experts in quitting. Now I know I have been talking about goals and perseverance, so how can happy people be great quitters? They are able to quit all the negative habits in their lives—things like smoking cigarettes, overeating, drinking too much, gambling too much, and watching too much television. A happy person does not like any habit to control them, especially negative habits.

We must do things because we truly desire to do them, not because we feel compelled to do them. Our lives today result from the choices we have made in the past. We can make better choices whenever we wish, and this often involves a lot of quitting. Sometimes we need to quit our repetitive negative thought processes, including putting ourselves down, worrying, being pessimistic, being afraid to try new things, being unambitious, and being ungrateful. Sometimes we need to quit our negative behaviors toward others, including being argumentative, inconsiderate, uncompassionate, rude, obnoxious, judgmental, and condescending.

Sometimes we even need to quit hanging around with people in our lives. Remember, we are our own best friends. If our friends are involved in negative behaviors and are not willing to change, it may be time to change our friends; otherwise, they just might change us! It is difficult to become a productive, positive person when we have negative, unproductive people always hanging around us; birds of a feather flock together!

We can see that to be happy, we need to become great quitters of the negative and champions of the positive!

Quit making bad choices, and do what is wise.
Quit harming yourself, and do what is healthy.
Quit behaving negatively, and do what is positive.
Quit making excuses,
do what your heart says.
Quit living a fantasy life
And become what you truly desire.

CHAPTER 26
AFFIRMATIONS

- I QUIT DOING THINGS THAT ARE HARMFUL TO ME.

- I QUIT TALKING DOWN TO MYSELF.

- I QUIT HOLDING RESENTMENT AND ANGER TOWARD OTHERS.

- I QUIT FEELING GUILTY FOR MY MISTAKES.

- I QUIT BEING AFRAID TO FOLLOW MY DREAMS.

- I QUIT HESITATING TO TAKE ACTION.

- I QUIT HAVING REGRETS FOR PAST CHOICES.

- I QUIT LIVING A LIFE WITHOUT PASSION.

- I QUIT COMPARING MYSELF TO THOSE AROUND ME.

- I QUIT FEELING BADLY ABOUT MYSELF.

27.
LEARN FROM FAILURE

Can we all win every time at everything we do? Of course not! It is absolutely unrealistic to think that we could; after all, we are only human. Sometimes we think of ourselves as superhuman, but this can bring us a lot of unhappiness. Many of us were brought up to put a lot of pressure on ourselves to become perfect. Though there is nothing wrong with striving to win, it is very dangerous to not be able to accept our own failures.

Failures are part of the learning process. It is impossible to learn anything of value without going through a little bit of adversity. As babies, we cried for hours before we learned how to communicate. As toddlers, we fell again and again as we learned how to walk. As children, we were corrected hundreds of times by our parents, before we learned right from wrong. Learning is always a process. We need to stop believing that failure is a bad thing and focus more on perseverance and determination. You know the old saying "practice makes perfect." It is true! Everything that is worth learning takes time, a little heartache, and a lot of patience.

When we have mastered something, we can feel pride and happiness in our accomplishment because of all the hard work and effort we put in. It is not easy to accept failure; it takes grace and humility (two very worthwhile characteristics). We should always remember that if we possess determination, failure is usually just the beginning of something, not the end of everything.

If you are afraid to fail, you may never be able to take the risks you need to succeed. You may end up always playing it safe, never living the life that you truly desire.

Failure is the great teacher.
It teaches us perseverance; it builds character.
It allows us to make wiser choices.
It is the doorway to success.

CHAPTER 27
AFFIRMATIONS

- I LEARN FROM MY FAILURES.

- I APPRECIATE MY MISTAKES.

- I KNOW MY PAST DOES NOT DETERMINE MY FUTURE.

- I KEEP TRYING UNTIL I GET IT RIGHT.

- I KNOW THAT TO ATTAIN SUCCESS, I CANNOT BE AFRAID TO FAIL.

- I KNOW DISCOVERY COMES FROM FAILING.

- I KNOW FAILING BRINGS ME ONE STEP CLOSER TO SUCCESS.

- I KNOW NEVER FAILING MEANS I NEVER ATTEMPTED.

- I KNOW FAILURE IS A PROCESS TO SUCCESS.

- I KNOW A LESSON LEARNED IS WORTH ITS WEIGHT IN GOLD.

28.
AVOID EGO TRIPS

Do you know the old saying "Pride goeth before a fall?" The kind of pride this refers to is the kind in which we believe we are somehow more important than everyone else and think we deserve more than others do. One of the reasons happy people are so happy is that they do not think they automatically deserve anything. They believe that nobody makes us any guarantees in life and that we have earned what we have learned. We reap what we sow!

Often, it may appear that arrogant people are extremely self-confident. Actually, they are just the opposite. They suffer from very low self-esteem and are very unhappy people. Unhappy people try to take out their unhappiness on everyone else. Perhaps the only satisfaction they can get out of life is from belittling those around them because they themselves feel so inadequate. Think about it: If you truly felt good about yourself, would you look down on others? Of course not. As we said before, happy people treat everyone with the same amount of respect and courtesy. It takes a truly happy and confident person to serve others. You can't be of much value to people if you are not happy with yourself.

Somewhere along the way, an ego trip will inevitably come to an abrupt and disappointing end. People who take ego trips are desperately trying to validate their self-worth in the eyes of others. Those of us with healthy egos simply look within and know we must earn respect by respecting others. The irony lies in the fact that only when we stop trying to prove to the rest of the world how important we are will they believe in us.

We are all unique;
We all have value.
No one is better than another;
No one is more important.
We discover ourselves
By experiencing others.

CHAPTER 28
AFFIRMATIONS

- I GAIN RESPECT BY RESPECTING OTHERS.

- I AM EQUAL TO BUT NOT GREATER THAN ANY OTHER PERSON.

- I KNOW THAT WE ALL BRING VALUE TO THE TABLE OF LIFE.

- I PREFER TO LOOK UP TO OTHERS RATHER THAN DOWN UPON THEM.

- I AM A TEAM MEMBER OF THE HUMAN RACE.

- I AM KIND TO EVERYONE AROUND ME.

- I ENJOY SERVING OTHERS.

- I EARN FROM WHAT I HAVE LEARNED.

- I AM ONLY AS WORTHY AS THE NEXT PERSON.

- I AM ALWAYS WILLING TO SHARE MY EXPERTISE.

29.
BELIEF

To accomplish anything, we must have belief. The good news is that we do not have to start out believing; belief grows stronger through the process of maintaining powerful desire. We must truly energetically desire what we are attempting to accomplish. If we do not, we will not succeed—or, even worse, we won't even try. Belief is the result of desire and is the most powerful form of thought on the planet.

Beliefs can sustain or squash innovative ideas, create or destroy nations, and help or harm lives. Beliefs do not always have to be positive to come true. We have seen our world's history shaped by many negative beliefs. The more emotional energy and desire we put behind our beliefs, the greater the possibility of them coming true. You might say that the key to belief is an emotionally charged desire—so be careful what you desire!

To become happy, we must first desire to achieve happiness. Many people are of the belief that they are doomed to lives of unhappiness. They do not dare to achieve happiness, because they are afraid of failing. In a very real sense, these unhappy people are applying the action of belief, without being aware of it. They truly believe that unhappiness is their fate, and because of this belief, they experience unhappiness.

Happy people have learned that they can be happy regardless of the situation they are in or even how grim the future might look. They have come to believe that they create their own happiness and maintaining it is within their reach. We must take many actions to live lives of happiness, but all those actions will be in vain without belief. If you try to start living a happier life but never come to the conclusion that happiness is your inalienable right, you will eventually lose confidence and give up when hardships appear. Start with a powerful desire that you can become happier, and a strong belief will certainly follow!

If I strongly desire to be happy,
I will then believe that I am happy,
And then I will become happy.
If I strongly desire to be loved,
I will then believe that I am loved,
And then I will become loved.
If I strongly desire to be successful,
I will then believe that I am successful,
And then I will become successful.
If I strongly desire to be healthy,
I will then believe that I am healthy,
And then I will become heathy.

CHAPTER 29
AFFIRMATIONS

- I KNOW THAT STRONG BELIEF IS THE RESULT OF STRONG DESIRE.

- I KNOW MY DESIRES CREATE THOUGHTS, WHICH RESULT IN BELIEFS.

- I KNOW WE ALL POSSESS UNIQUE BELIEFS.

- I KNOW THAT MY BELIEFS ARE THE SUMMATION OF MY IMAGINATION.

- I CHANGE NEGATIVE BELIEFS BY OBTAINING NEW DESIRES.

- I DO NOT HAVE TO BELIEVE WHEN I FIRST DESIRE TO ACHIEVE.

- I KNOW THE ACT OF DESIRING LEADS TO BELIEF.

- I PERIODICALLY CRITIQUE MY BELIEFS.

- I KNOW THAT COLLABORATION FOSTERS GREATER BELIEF.

- I KNOW THAT BELIEF GROWS LIKE A PLANT FROM A SEED.

30.
TAKE RESPONSIBILITY

Is someone or something other than ourselves responsible for our own happiness? According to happy people, the answer is clearly no! We, and we alone, are 100 percent responsible for our own happiness! Happiness is an attitude and a state of mind that is the result of many varied thoughts and behaviors that we personally control and create throughout our lives. Unless we believe this to be true, we may never experience the joy that is rightfully ours.

Happiness is not somewhere over the rainbow; it is an attitude that we can maintain. Happiness just doesn't happen automatically; we need to apply consistent positive habits for happiness to exist. Think about it: When you try to make someone else happy, is there work involved? Of course. Why, then, should it be any different with ourselves?

We all experience difficult situations in life, some situations more painful than others. Some of us must overcome more adversity than others.

Many of us wish to blame everything but ourselves for our feelings of unhappiness. We may not be able to control the things that happen to us, but we can always control the way we handle them. No one ever promised that life would be fair. It is natural for us to feel sorry for ourselves when difficulties arise. Others may offer a certain amount of sympathy and compassion, but they won't do so forever. Because we, and we alone, are responsible for our thoughts, behaviors, and emotions, it is up to us to experience our difficulties, overcome them, then let go and move on to discover ways to create renewed joy and happiness.

Remember, many roads lead to happiness, not just one.

I decide to get up out of bed.
I decide what attitude I will have.
I decide how I will react today.
I decide what kind of effort I will put forth.
I decide my level of happiness.
I decide my degree of success.
I decide the kind of life that I will lead.

CHAPTER 30
AFFIRMATIONS

- I TAKE SOLE RESPONSIBILITY FOR MY HAPPINESS.

- I KNOW THAT HAPPINESS STARTS FROM THE INSIDE.

- I GENERATE MY OWN HAPPINESS

- I CHOOSE TO FEEL HAPPY AND THANKFUL.

- I KNOW THAT HAPPINESS PERPETUATES HAPPINESS.

- I FEEL THE MOMENTUM OF HAPPINESS.

- I KNOW HAPPY THOUGHTS TRANSFORM INTO HAPPY FEELINGS.

- I AM RESPONSIBLE FOR ONLY MY OWN HAPPINESS.

- I TAKE FULL OWNERSHIP OF MY CURRENT SITUATION.

- I DO NOT ALLOW OTHERS TO CONTROL MY HAPPINESS.

31.
COURAGEOUS LIVING

Happy people experience a lot less fear in their lives than unhappy people do. The nature of a large portion of unhappiness is fear, worry, and anxiety. Unhappy people review a never-ending stream of detailed mental videos that display all the possible negative scenarios that could conceivably appear in their lives. In contrast, happy people continuously imagine all of the positive possibilities that could appear in their lives.

Most of us would probably save about three hours a day if we could stop worrying about things that haven't even happened. This worry destroys happiness.

When we can learn to trust in our coping skills, we can release ourselves from the sickness of worry and can learn to solve our issues as they arise.

It takes courage to live a fulfilling, productive, and happy life, and to grab the bull by the horns and follow your dreams. We all experience fear, but are you going to let fear prevent you from living a life of your own design?

Turn your fears into positive thinking; turn your worries into positive thoughts; and turn your anxieties into positive actions. An optimist has no time for fear; a planner has no time to worry, and a doer has no time to be anxious.

We can either stick our heads in the sand for the rest of our lives or get out there and face our fears and experience what life has to offer. The quickest way to become more courageous is to directly confront your fears. When we confront our fears, we usually discover that they were not quite as scary as we had thought. It takes an enormous amount of work, bravery, and courage to love, to learn, to support a family, to meet life's challenges, to continue to improve, and to follow our desires and ambitions, but it is definitely worth the effort.

It can take away my ambition;
It can destroy my self-esteem.
It can ruin my relationships;
It can prevent me from succeeding.
It can stop me from improving;
It can squelch all my desires.
It can force me to give up on my dreams;
It can take away all my happiness.
It is fear.

CHAPTER 31
AFFIRMATIONS

- I AM BRAVE AND COURAGEOUS.

- I FIGHT THROUGH MY FEARS.

- I KNOW OPTIMISM REMOVES ALL DOUBT.

- I WOULD RATHER FAIL THAN NEVER TRY.

- I KNOW COURAGE GROWS WITH POSITIVE RESULTS.

- I AM MY OWN HERO.

- I WILL TAKE ACTION, BECAUSE IF I DO NOT, I WILL REMAIN IN THE SAME STATE.

- I TRUST IN MYSELF ENOUGH TO REMAIN COURAGEOUS.

- I IMAGINE POSITIVE OUTCOMES.

- I ANTICIPATE EXCELLENCE AND GREATNESS FROM MYSELF.

32.
SELF-ACCEPTANCE

To lead happy lives, we must learn to accept ourselves. Most of us spend a lot of mental energy worrying about what others are thinking and saying about us but very little mental energy thinking about how we feel about ourselves. If we attempt to spend the rest of our lives trying to please everyone around us in order to gain their approval, we will be destined to lives of sadness and disappointment. People can be fickle and opinionated; they may like you today but decide tomorrow that they don't like you at all. Do you really want to spend the rest of your life jumping through hoops trying to please the world? It is a no-win situation, because it is absolutely impossible to please everyone. The bottom line is that the only acceptance that we should truly seek is our own.

We need to love and value ourselves for who we are and not because of how others perceive us. Only when we accept ourselves for the unique individuals we are can we sincerely accept others for who they are. We are all born with no greater or lesser value than any other human. We are all worthy of respect and acceptance, and though we may not be able to get it from the rest of the world, we can certainly learn to give it to ourselves.

To experience happiness, we must learn to separate who we are from how we perform. The world will usually judge us on our performance, but when we accept ourselves, it should always be based on who we are. If we base our self-acceptance on how we perform, we will feel good about ourselves only when we are performing well—so what happens when we are not performing well? Happiness involves learning to unconditionally love and accept ourselves for the wonderfully unique people that we are.

I accept myself unconditionally.
I accept myself for who I am now;
I accept myself for who I was then.
I accept myself for who
I will become.

CHAPTER 32
AFFIRMATIONS

- I ACCEPT MYSELF UNCONDITIONALLY.

- I AM MY NUMBER-ONE ALLY.

- I AM THE PRESIDENT OF MY OWN FAN CLUB.

- I BELIEVE IN MYSELF AND MY ABILITIES.

- I ACCEPT MY WEAKNESSES AND STRIVE TO STRENGTHEN THEM.

- I TRUST IN MY OPINIONS AND CONCLUSIONS.

- I EMBRACE MY UNIQUENESS.

- I ENJOY THE PRIVILEGE OF BEING ALIVE.

- I AM GRATEFUL FOR MY PAST MISTAKES.

- I TRULY LIKE MYSELF.

33.
UNDERSTANDING

Happy people strive to understand others more than they strive to be understood. Have you ever noticed how unhappy people are always worrying about how they were misunderstood, were not understood, or didn't fit in with everyone else?

We all wish to be understood; that is part of human nature. I wouldn't be a very good writer if I didn't care to be understood. In fact, I probably wouldn't be a writer at all— why bother? Happy people are confident within themselves, so they don't feel or think that the world must revolve around them.

When we are happy, we realize that when people appear to misunderstand us, that may not be the case. Most people aren't thinking about us at all; they are thinking about their own lives and problems, so what may look like a slight to us is someone dealing with their own issues, without regard to ours.

Happy people can offer a lot to those who haven't figured out how to allow themselves happiness in their own lives. This involves more listening than talking, more acceptance than judgment, and more understanding than being understood.

One of the greatest gifts we can give a person is the gift of feedback. Many people don't really know themselves. When we can help others to clarify their thinking or sort through their emotions, we can help them to better understand themselves.

Happy people believe that if they are misunderstood, it is probably due to poor communication on their part, or they realize that the audience is not ready or capable of understanding them. Happy people don't get down on themselves for not being understood; they usually just try harder to understand.

I will strive to understand
More than I will seek to be understood.
I will listen more to others
And talk less about myself.
I will respect the freedom of every individual
And not insist that they accept all of my views.

CHAPTER 33
AFFIRMATIONS

- I SEEK TO UNDERSTAND RATHER THAN TO JUDGE.

- I VIEW ALL SIDES OF EVERY SITUATION.

- I FEEL EMPATHY AND COMPASSION FOR OTHERS.

- I STUDY THE MOTIVES BEHIND PEOPLE'S ACTIONS.

- I KNOW PEACE COMES FROM UNDERSTANDING.

- I LISTEN TO OTHERS WITH MY HEART.

- I KNOW THAT EVERYONE HAS A STORY TO TELL.

- I KNOW THAT PEOPLE HAVE DIVERSE STYLES OF COMMUNICATION.

- I ASK OTHERS TO HELP ME UNDERSTAND THEIR FEELINGS.

- I LISTEN TO UNDERSTAND.

34.
SLOW AND STEADY

My inspiration for this chapter is the old joke "How do you eat an elephant?" (the answer: one piece at a time). How do you change your life? Slowly and steadily, one action at a time. Think about a large ship traveling across the ocean. If we were to move the rudder even one tenth of a degree in either direction, we would change our course, and eventually, we would completely change our destination. A drop of water doesn't seem like much water at all, but if I were able to make a large room watertight, close the sink drain, and turn on the faucet so one drop of water came out every few seconds, eventually, the room would be flooded. These two analogies demonstrate that small, steady changes add up to large, dramatic results.

We live in a society of instant gratification, and we are not always willing to put in the hard work necessary to achieve our goals. We did not develop unhappy lives overnight, so why should we think we can make everything better overnight? It takes a long time to develop an unhappy life, and it is safe to conclude that it will take a respectable amount of time to reverse the damage.

Remember that small, steady changes always add up to large, dramatic results. Begin with one small positive change in your life and see it through. There is no telling where one small, steady positive change will take you, though I am certain it will be a better place. Small, steady changes create enormous momentum, and when we finally do see results, we become even more motivated to make more positive changes. Don't let the size of the elephant in your life prevent you from taking action. Remember, slow and steady, one moment at a time!

Step by step,
Moment by moment,
One thought at a time,
One action at a time
Propels us forward,
Away from the past
And into the future.
Small, steady changes
Create large, dramatic results.

CHAPTER 34
AFFIRMATIONS

- I KNOW SMALL CHANGES LEAD TO GREAT ACCOM-PLISHMENTS.

- I KNOW EVERY POSITIVE ACTION LEADS TO A BENE-FICIAL CHANGE.

- I WILL WIN THE RACE, REGARDLESS OF HOW FAST I FINISH.

- I SET WISE TIME FRAMES FOR MY GOALS.

- I KNOW A TINY THOUGHT CAN CREATE AN ENORMOUS CHANGE IN DIRECTION.

- I AM PATIENT WITH MYSELF.

- I CLIMB TO THE TOP ONE STEP AT A TIME.

- I REACH MY DESTINATION WITH MANY STOPS ALONG THE WAY.

- I HAVE MOMENTUM ON MY SIDE.

- I APPRECIATE THE MOMENTS ON THE WAY TO MY DESIRES.

35.
WE ARE NOT MULES

We are not mules. We are not meant to take on other people's burdens. We were not built for it. We must take care of our own burdens in order to become productive members of society.

It is one thing to help our fellow man, but it is quite another to carry his load for him. Happy people are helpful people, but they do not let themselves take on other people's problems. They realize that everyone must struggle and carry their own share of the weight. This is part of the learning curve in life: We are not really helping people by taking over their problems; we are only helping them feel that they are inadequate by depending on us.

Happy people try to become independent people, whereas unhappy people seem to be dependent on everyone but themselves. Part of becoming a happy person is learning that we must not depend on outside forces to gain happiness. We must realize that happiness comes from within. Unfortunately, there are many manipulative people in this world who will try to make us feel guilty and responsible for all of their personal issues and misfortunes. They will try every trick in the book to make us become their mules and would like nothing better than to watch us carry their loads while they sit back in the shade somewhere and relax. Be wary of these mule-making manipulators; they will use you for all you are worth and then leave you to clean up their mess.

Happy people have learned through failure that they cannot help anyone who does not wish to help him/herself. If we think we can help others who don't want to help themselves, we are simply nurturing our own egos.

Lend a hand, give advice, listen, be charitable with your time and money, but try not to solve everyone else's problems for them; there is usually more than enough trouble for us right in our own backyards.

Solving people's problems for them
May not always be the best policy.
Helping others to help themselves
Is usually the wisest action.

CHAPTER 35
AFFIRMATIONS

- I AM TRULY RESPONSIBLE FOR ONLY MYSELF.

- I OFFER OTHERS ASSISTANCE, NOT SOLUTIONS.

- I KNOW EVERYONE MUST CARRY THEIR OWN WEIGHT.

- I AM NOT HELPING OTHERS WHEN I TAKE ON THEIR PROBLEMS.

- I ENJOY HELPING THOSE WHO LIKE TO HELP THEM- SELVES.

- I KNOW EVERYONE MUST PARTICIPATE IN THEIR OWN JOURNEYS.

- I KNOW THAT A SPIRIT OF TEAMWORK IS INFECTIOUS.

- I WILL DO MY PART TO HELP OTHERS DO THEIR PARTS.

- I KNOW THAT WE MUST ALL EARN OUR OWN OUT- COMES.

- I AM ABLE TO TEACH ONLY THOSE WHO DESIRE TO LEARN.

36.
CONTROL YOUR ANGER

Happy people admit that anger is a valid emotion. No matter how much happiness we have in our lives, we will always have moments when we become angry with someone or something, even ourselves. The most popular belief about anger is that it should be avoided and suppressed at all costs. On the contrary, happy people believe that anger should be confronted and dealt with head-on. There is nothing innately wrong with the emotion of anger. We were all created with this emotion for a reason.

What possible positive benefit can anger have for us? It is designed to protect us when we feel threatened. Originally, it prepared our bodies physically ready for defensive battle by pumping adrenaline throughout our systems and heightening our senses. We didn't always live in a civilized world, so anger was more useful and necessary for our ancestors than it is today.

In today's world, we cannot indulge in our anger emotion whenever, wherever, and however we feel the urge. That would only result in extremely negative outcomes. We need to learn to harness our anger if we are to live happy and fulfilling lives.

The next time you experience anger, before you do something you will more than likely regret, try slowing down by taking deep breaths and then try to figure out what your anger is trying to tell you. Remember, we get angry only when we feel threatened in some way. The threat may not actually be real, but it may seem real. We need to try to figure out the source of our anger and deal with it in a mature manner. It is not beneficial to deny our anger, but it is not wise to let it become out of control.

Don't avoid your anger.
Listen to your anger.
What is it telling you?
Do you feel threatened?
Is it valid?
Experience your anger.
Learn from your anger
But Try to control it.

CHAPTER 36
AFFIRMATIONS

- I INVESTIGATE MY ANGER AS IT ARISES.

- I STEP AWAY FROM MY ANGER.

- I ACT ONLY WHEN MY ANGER HAS SUBSIDED.

- I AM IN CONTROL OF MY EMOTIONS.

- I LEARN FROM MY INTERNAL EMOTIONAL STATES.

- I HARNESS MY ANGER FOR POSITIVE GAINS.

- I LET MYSELF EXPRESS ANGER IN A CONTROLLED MANNER.

- I KNOW ANGER APPEARS IN THE WORD DANGER.

- I KNOW LONG-TERM ANGER IS POISONOUS TO MY BODY.

- I KNOW FORGIVENESS REMOVES ANGER.

37.
STAY FOCUSED

Life is like a giant buffet—there are many choices. If you have ever tried to eat a little bit of everything on the food buffet (like I have), you know how miserable you felt when you were finished. Although all the tasty treats on the buffet look good, they are not necessarily all good for us. We cannot indulge in everything that life has to offer; it is neither beneficial nor possible.

Happy people live focused lives. They don't just jump from one thing to the next in an irrational manner; they make well-informed and educated decisions. They plan out their lives by writing down their goals and discovering their ultimate purpose.

Happy people are organized and stay on track so they can reach the destinations they have chosen. They do not let life determine their outcomes but determine the outcomes of their own lives instead.

We can be easily distracted by all the options that today's world presents us, but we must realize that we should not always do something just because we can! I am not saying that happy people are so rigid that they cannot allow for any spontaneity in their lives—they realize that allowing for spontaneity is beneficial—but living a life of pure spontaneity is extremely unproductive.

Sometimes we feel like the responsibilities in our lives are overwhelming, and we are tempted to hide or to run away. When life gets too stressful, we tend to create fantasies of how much greener the grass is on the other side. Just remember that the grass on our side looks green from the other side as well; there is no perfect place or situation on Earth. All we can do is try to create, through careful planning and intelligent choices, the most satisfying and rewarding lives we possibly can.

Tend to your life like a garden;
Plant positive seeds.
Water it, prune it;
Remove all the weeds,
And watch it flourish!

CHAPTER 37
AFFIRMATIONS

- I AM LASER-FOCUSED ON MY GOALS.

- I CAREFULLY CONSIDER ALL OF MY OPTIONS.

- I MAKE CHOICES THAT LEAD TO BENEFICIAL OUT-COMES.

- I METICULOUSLY DEFINE MY DESIRES.

- I STICK TO MY PLANS WHILE ALLOWING ROOM FOR ADAPTATIONS.

- I MAKE WISE DECISIONS THAT ARE WELL THOUGHT OUT.

- I WEED NEGATIVE PEOPLE FROM MY LIFE.

- I HANG AROUND WITH AMBITIOUS PEOPLE.

- I FOCUS ON WHAT I AM DOING IN THE MOMENT.

- I FOCUS ON BOTH THE DETAILS AND THE BIG PIC-TURE.

38.
SAVE THE BEST FOR LAST

This chapter is all about procrastination. I don't mind telling you that for some reason, I kept putting it off. (That's my attempt at humor.)

We all have responsibilities in life; some of them we enjoy, and some of them, we don't. We don't hesitate to do tasks we enjoy, because they are not work. For example, I love to write. Although it is a task to complete an entire book that I can be proud of, I don't consider it work, because it gives me so much enjoyment. If I didn't have other responsibilities, I would probably write for the majority of my day—but I do have other responsibilities. First, I get all the things out of the way that I would rather not do, so I can look forward to the best thing.

We procrastinate only on things that we would rather avoid. We usually feel guilty when we procrastinate, because we tend to blame ourselves for being lazy or unmotivated. We should not feel guilty, however, because it is impossible to become enthusiastic or motivated about something that we have no interest in doing. Instead of trying to motivate ourselves, we should admit that we don't like the task ahead of us but face that we must do it so we can get to the things we like to do. The result of saving the best for last is that we commit to doing the things we would rather avoid, and thus, we stop procrastinating.

Unhappy people tend to procrastinate. A lot of our unhappiness comes from our lives being unorganized and out of control because of procrastination. The things we don't like to do are still things that need to be done. I dislike mowing the lawn and shopping for clothing, but if I didn't do those things, I would eventually become a naked guy with an ugly lawn, and this would make my neighbors and me both very unhappy!

Work is called work for a reason;
Some things just need to be done.
Finish your chores during the day
So you can play in the evening.
Procrastination doesn't get us out of work;
It only delays the inevitable.
I would rather face a mole's hill
Than a mountain.
There is a great sense of freedom
In finishing an unpleasant task
To make room for what we enjoy.

CHAPTER 38
AFFIRMATIONS

- I GET THINGS DONE!

- I REWARD MYSELF AFTER A JOB WELL DONE.

- I QUICKLY AND EFFECTIVELY KNOCK OUT ANNOYING TASKS.

- I PUT OFF FUN UNTIL THE WORK IS DONE.

- I STAY ON TOP OF MY DAY.

- I CREATE A PLAN AND THEN WORK MY PLAN.

- I KNOW NOTHING GOOD COMES WITHOUT SOME HARD WORK.

- I DO WHAT I WANT WHEN I'VE DONE WHAT I MUST.

- I HIRE OTHERS TO COMPLETE SOME OF MY UNDESIRABLE TASKS.

- I CREATE ROOM IN MY SCHEDULE FOR UNEXPECTED EVENTS.

39.
FOLLOW YOUR DREAMS

We all have dreams and visions for the ways we wish to live our lives. The question is, do we follow those dreams or give up on them? We are sometimes told that dreams are only for the young and naïve and that adults are much more mature and realistic. Who tells us this? Usually, it is people who have given up on their dreams, because using this excuse makes them feel better about themselves. But being mature and realistic is a great asset for when you are actually *pursuing* your dreams.

Young people might have more uninhibited imaginations, but maturity offers us the wisdom to get the job done. So why do we give up on our dreams? Usually, we start with negative beliefs: We are afraid of failure, are scared of success, cannot deal with obstacles, think we are not worthy of success, are worried what others may think, or feel that we don't have what it takes to accomplish our goals. These are valid emotional concerns that we may face, but they are not legitimate reasons for us to give up on following our dreams. The only legitimate reason for giving up on our dreams is deciding that those dreams were what we thought we wanted but really weren't.

We can focus on our negative beliefs, or we can work through them by keeping our eyes on our vision. The choice is ours. No one has ever followed a dream without running into obstacles or without feeling like quitting a time or two. The gold at the end of the rainbow is usually found after an arduous journey, but if we give up on the journey altogether, we will always look back and wonder if we could have made it. If we give up on the journey, we may end up leading lives of complacency because we did not follow our passions.

Follow your dreams and face difficulties, or quit and possibly live a life filled with regrets—which road will you choose?

We are each given one shot at living.
We are each called to one major purpose.
We are each granted specific talents;
We are each born with unique abilities.
We are each aware of our dreams;
We are each able to follow them.

CHAPTER 39
AFFIRMATIONS

- I WILL SURRENDER ONLY TO SUCCESS.

- I WILL FOLLOW MY DREAMS TO COMPLETION.

- I WILL LIVE A LIFE OF PASSION.

- I WILL REMAIN ON THE RIGHT TRACK.

- I WILL DREAM AS BIG AS HUMANLY POSSIBLE.

- I KNOW PASSION CREATES ACTION.

- I WILL ASK A LOT FROM MYSELF.

- I AM INSPIRED TO REACH GREAT HEIGHTS.

- I DESIGN THE LIFE THAT I WISH TO LIVE.

- I WILL HELP OTHERS ACHIEVE THEIR DREAMS.

40.
EXPERIENCE THE MOMENTS

When it comes right down to it, our lives are made up of a series of moments. We get so caught up in our own issues that we forget to relax and to take time to enjoy all of the wonderful moments happening around us. It's like each of us leads two lives: the one going on around us and the mental one in which a running commentary analyzes and dissects everything.

We try to analyze everything because we want to be able to capture the moments in life with thoughts and words, much like a camera captures a photograph. The problem lies in the fact that we can't really capture moments as well as we can experience them. We don't need to explain, label, or describe everything. Sometimes the lesson in life is in the moment itself and doesn't need anything added to it. Which would you rather experience, the beauty of a butterfly in flight or a butterfly that is captured and pinned up behind a glass frame? We cannot frame all our moments in glass and hang them on our walls. If we could do that, we would spend all our time looking at the past, which would prevent us from experiencing the present.

Life has a lot of wonderful moments that can bring us great happiness and joy if we are willing to pay attention to them. How many moments of happiness can we grab out of a day? There is certainly an unlimited supply of beauty and wonder in this world; there is nothing quite as beautiful as the smile of a baby, the sky at sunset, the feel of a cool breeze as it rushes across our face, the smell of a freshly baked pie, or the company of someone you love. Remember, happiness is not a constant, but the more wonderful moments we experience, the more happiness we will find.

Many moments surround us.
Focus on those
That create the most joy.

CHAPTER 40
AFFIRMATIONS

- I KNOW A FOOTSTEP'S TIME HAS A MILLION MOMENTS.

- I EXPERIENCE THE JOY IN EACH MOMENT.

- I ENJOY THE RIDE ON THE WAY TO THE DESTINATION.

- I KNOW LIFE IS A SERIES OF MOMENTS.

- I LEAVE EACH EXPERIENCE FOR THE NEXT.

- I KNOW A SIMPLE MOMENT CAN HAVE A PROFOUND EFFECT.

- I CREATE MOMENTUM MOMENT BY MOMENT.

- I LIVE BY THE MOMENT BUT PLAN FOR THE FUTURE.

- I TAKE THE TIME TO REVIEW THE SPECIAL MOMENTS.

- I AM GRATEFUL FOR EACH AND EVERY MOMENT OF MY LIFE.

41.
MAKE ROOM FOR PLAY

We will always find the time to earn a living. Without work, it would be very difficult to survive in this world, because we need money to survive and to take care of our basic needs, such as health, shelter, safety, food, and clothing. We will usually put work above other things in our lives, however, and this can become a great source of unhappiness.

Our lives are made up of many pieces, like a giant jigsaw puzzle. Although work is a very important piece, it is not the only piece. I think we would all agree that a one-piece jigsaw puzzle would become extremely dull and boring—but that is exactly what can become of us if we continue to be all work and no play!

No matter how important our responsibilities, we need to make room for play. We need to spend time with our families and friends and, most of all, our children! We need to become well-rounded people with varied interests and hobbies. We need to make time to relax and to renew our minds. We need to know how to take breaks and have a little fun. Happy people make room for play, and they know that people who work all the time will eventually accomplish less than those who take time out regularly to enjoy life.

If we played all the time and hardly worked, we would also end up with very unhappy lives, because everything that is one-sided inevitably collapses. We need to keep everything in perspective; work allows us to play, and play allows us to be more productive workers. Happiness involves a lot of balance and moderation.

Give yourself a break.
Don't forget to enjoy life;
Your work will still be there
When you return from playing.
We tell ourselves that we work so hard
So we can take care of our families,
But if our families never see us,
We are not truly taking care of them.
We need to balance work and play;
This creates an awesome lifestyle.

CHAPTER 41
AFFIRMATIONS

- I TAKE SOME TIME TO HAVE FUN.

- I LOVE TO HANG OUT WITH FAMILY AND FRIENDS.

- I AM ABLE TO RELAX AND RENEW MY MIND.

- I MAKE SURE I ENJOY THE FRUITS OF MY LABOR.

- I AM NEVER TOO OLD FOR A PLAYDATE.

- I LOVE TO SIMPLY GOOF OFF SOMETIMES.

- I MAKE ROOM FOR SPONTANEITY IN MY LIFE.

- I TAKE FREQUENT SHORT MENTAL BREAKS.

- I ENJOY TAKING SMALL GETAWAYS

- I BALANCE MY WORK LIFE AND PLAYTIME.

42.
LEARN TO LAUGH

Happy people realize that laughter really is the best medicine. Laughter releases tons of tension in our bodies and can help us relax during times of stress. It can also refresh our minds by changing our emotional states, which can usually allow us to see things in a new light. Laughter just plain feels good; certain chemicals in our brains are released when we laugh and improve our moods. If we take life too seriously, we will eventually destroy our chance at happiness. We all need an emotional escape every now and then—one that has a positive effect on our minds and is harmless to our bodies. Laughter is the solution.

To experience laughter, we must give ourselves permission to let go and be silly. We often spend so much time and energy trying to keep up our self-important images that we forget how to let our guards down and just have a good time. I think laughter is the secret ingredient in the fountain of youth; it keeps us young at heart and prevents us from becoming permanently cynical about life. We also look younger and have more energy when we enjoy laughter regularly. The medicine of laughter dissolves and diffuses many negative emotions and behaviors such as fear, depression, boredom, embarrassment, and anger.

We can usually look back and find some kind of humor in almost every difficult situation. Perhaps laughter is the mysterious elixir that prevents us from completely losing our sanity, especially in those times when the loss of our sanity seems inevitable. We may not have all been blessed with the talent of being able to make other people laugh, but we were all born with the ability to experience and enjoy laughter.

It relaxes our bodies;
It purifies our souls.
It keeps our minds positive;
It smooths out rough edges.
It's among the sounds of playing children.
It defeats anger;
It kills boredom.
It allows us to remain young.
It breeds courage;
It feels good.
It is laughter.

CHAPTER 42
AFFIRMATIONS

- I KNOW LAUGHTER IS TRULY THE BEST MEDICINE.

- I ALLOW ROOM FOR LAUGHTER IN MY LIFE.

- I AM NEVER TOO BUSY TO HAVE A GOOD LAUGH.

- I KNOW A SENSE OF HUMOR KEEPS ME GROUNDED.

- I KNOW THAT A LIGHTHEARTED NATURE ACCOMPLISHES MORE.

- I LOVE WATCHING FUNNY MOVIES AND TELEVISION SHOWS.

- I ASPIRE NOT TO TAKE MYSELF TOO SERIOUSLY.

- I LOVE THE SOUND OF LAUGHTER.

- I KNOW FREQUENT LAUGHTER CREATES A YOUTHFUL APPEARANCE.

- I CAN UNCOVER THE HUMOR EVEN IN DIFFICULT SITUATIONS.

43.
NO REGRETS

When the big hand on the clock moves one click forward, that previous second becomes the past. Once the past is set, there is no changing it; history cannot be rewritten. Your personal history, for better or worse, will remain the same and makes you who you are today.

Many of us suffer from unhappiness because we regret our past; we wish we had made different choices, or perhaps we feel guilty, angry, or sad about things we have done. Happy people also look back and see areas where they could have done things differently, but instead of dwelling on regret, they use this awareness to make better decisions in the future.

Happy people know that regret is a waste of time because regret doesn't change or accomplish a thing. We don't need to wallow in self-pity; we simply need to learn from our mistakes. Always remember that your past has created your current situation. If you don't like your present situation, you can change your future by making different choices here and now. In other words, we all have the ability to clean up our own messes if we choose to do so!

Perhaps in some twisted sense, we like to wear our regrets like badges of dishonor to show the world that we are not worthy of any happiness. In this way, we can avoid further guilt by getting attention, love, and sympathy from others without feeling like we strived for it.

The best policy, however, is to accept the past instead of punishing ourselves for it. We are always evolving in our levels of knowledge and maturity; this is the natural result of living. Why should we keep beating ourselves up about our past poor behavior or lack of wisdom? Just as we show forgiveness and acceptance to others regularly, we should extend this courtesy to ourselves.

We cannot move forward
If we are always looking backward.
We know where we have been;
Let's focus on where we are headed.

CHAPTER 43
AFFIRMATIONS

- I KNOW THE PAST DOES NOT PREDICT MY FUTURE.

- I LOOK BACK ONLY FOR THE LESSONS.

- I KNOW IT'S FRUITLESS TO JUDGE A YOUNGER, LESS-INFORMED ME.

- I CAN REDIRECT ONLY MY PRESENT CHOICES.

- I DWELL ON THE FUTURE BUT NOT MY PAST.

- I USE THE PAST AS A SPRINGBOARD TO THE FUTURE.

- I THINK ABOUT WHAT I WANT TO BECOME RATHER THAN WHAT I HAVE BEEN.

- I AM ALWAYS–ALWAYS–EVOLVING!

- I AM A WORK IN PROGRESS UNTIL THE END OF MY DAYS.

- I KNOW THE PAST HAS SHAPED ME, BUT THE MOLD CAN ALWAYS BE BROKEN.

44.
SCHOOL IS NEVER OUT

The fact that we have graduated from high school, college, or graduate school does not mean that we have stopped learning. We learn throughout our lives. It is not something that ends with formal education, although many people stop trying to learn new things after this point and rely on what they are told by media, friends, business associates, and society in general instead of putting in the time to research and find their own answers. Although there is nothing unethical about relying on these things, they do not always provide the most accurate information. If we do rely on others to obtain our information, we must do our own research to determine if the information is reliable.

Knowledge is useless without application. If we apply inaccurate information in our lives, we are bound to make incorrect decisions and bad choices. We must take sole responsibility for our continued education. The worst thing we can do is blindly accept everything we hear as the truth.

We all learn in different ways, so the only correct way for you to learn is the way that works for you! Learning is to the mind as exercising is to the muscles; learning new things keeps us excited and enthusiastic about life. It keeps our minds stimulated and our thought processes fresh and alive. It also strengthens our concentration as well as builds up our self-confidence.

Remember, we can collect all the information we desire, but unless we apply it to our lives, it is virtually useless. We are not reference guides that contain information but people who use information to transform our dreams into reality.

Life is an ongoing process.
From birth to death, we never stop maturing;
We never stop learning;
We never stop seeking.
We never stop evolving.

CHAPTER 44
AFFIRMATIONS

- I KNOW THAT LEARNING FUELS MY ENTHUSIASM.

- I SEEK TO LEARN SOMETHING NEW EVERY DAY.

- I AM NEVER TOO OLD TO LEARN SOMETHING NEW.

- I OPEN MY MIND TO NEW WAYS OF DOING THINGS.

- I KNOW KNOWLEDGE IS ONE OF THE MAJOR KEYS TO SUCCESS.

- I KNOW THAT I HAVE TRULY LEARNED WHEN I AM ABLE TO APPLY INFORMATION I HAVE GAINED.

- I ENJOY LEARNING MORE WHEN I HAVE A DEEP INTEREST IN THE SUBJECT.

- I KNOW THE REAL SCHOOLING BEGINS AFTER THE END OF MY FORMAL EDUCATION.

- I KNOW THE FIRST STEP IN ATTAINING WISDOM IS HAVING A CURIOUS MIND.

- I KNOW THAT INCREASING MY WISDOM PROPELS ME TO MAKE SMARTER CHOICES.

45.
VALUE YOUR PRIVACY

I am proud that I live in such a free society. One freedom that brings me a lot of happiness is my right to privacy. I have found that there is a correlation between happiness and using discretion in what we share with others. Some people just can't help blurting out all of their personal problems to everyone they come across, though this is often inappropriate with mere acquaintances. These days, for safety reasons alone, we need to place a high value on our privacy.

Unfortunately, we can't trust everyone we meet. We wouldn't dream of giving the keys to our houses or cars to strangers, so why do we hand over personal information about ourselves to anyone willing to listen? Some people aren't ethical and may use the information to discredit us or manipulate us in some manner. This is why it is a good policy to make sure someone has earned your trust before you provide them important information about yourself.

We also need our privacy to refresh our spirits and to keep our sanity intact. Sometimes we don't realize the true value of things until they are taken away. I learned all about this when I was a young man in the United States Navy. I lived on a ship for two years and had absolutely no privacy. I slept on a mattress the size of a coffin in a triple bunk bed, in a room with more than sixty people. I had a locker that was just slightly bigger than the average gym locker to store all my worldly possessions. There were no shower curtains, and in some cases, there weren't even doors on the toilet stalls. When I got out of the Navy, the thing I cherished most was getting my privacy back.

Sometimes we may need to be alone.
We need personal space
To rekindle our spirits,
To refresh our mental processes.
We are the private owners of our lives;
We control who we let into our worlds.
Our tongues are the gatekeepers
Controlling our privacy.

CHAPTER 45
AFFIRMATIONS

- I PLACE A HIGH VALUE ON MY PRIVACY.

- I RESPECT THE BOUNDARIES OF MYSELF AND OTHERS.

- I KNOW MY TONGUE IS THE GATEKEEPER OF MY PRIVACY.

- I NEED TIME ALONE TO RENEW MY SPIRIT.

- I SHARE PERSONAL FEELINGS ONLY WITH PEOPLE I TRUST.

- I HAVE A HIGH FENCE AROUND MY INNER SANCTUARY.

- I GIVE THE KEY TO MY SOUL ONLY TO THOSE WHO ARE WORTHY.

- I ENJOY SPENDING TIME WITH MYSELF.

- I KNOW EVERYONE DOES NOT NEED TO KNOW EVERYTHING ABOUT ME.

- I AM UNDER NO OBLIGATION TO ANSWER ANYONE'S QUESTIONS.

46.
PERSONAL INTEGRITY

Having personal integrity means doing the right thing according to our own standards and values, even when no one else is paying attention. When we have personal integrity, even if we have the opportunity to get away with something outside the scope of our sense of right and wrong, we will not take it.

Happy people live lives of personal integrity. They live by highly developed personal standards. Living lives of integrity grants us happiness. It provides us with a sense of guidance and security, and it gives us a roadmap for our behavior and a template for making some tough decisions. A person with integrity will try to live a life that is as honest and fair to themselves and everyone around them as is humanly possible.

Personal integrity is not the same as situational ethics. In other words, when we have personal integrity, we don't follow a different set of guidelines based on what is happening around us. It also means that we don't reciprocate honesty only to those who are honest to us but remain honest with everyone, no matter how they treat us.

To act with personal integrity, one must first know what their personal standards and values are all about; your parents likely helped shape and mold your standards and values. At some point in our lives, we all need to sit down and reevaluate our personal standards to make sure that we are completely satisfied with them. Remember, this is all about personal integrity, not about doing and believing what everyone else tells you is right or wrong.

I really enjoy my sense of integrity. It has given me a track to run on, and life is a lot easier when I know which lane to stay in.

Personal integrity is
A roadmap for our behavior,
The compass to our choices,
And the telescope to our future.

CHAPTER 46
AFFIRMATIONS

- I DECIDE THE THINGS I WILL CONFORM TO.

- I ADHERE TO MY OWN SET OF STANDARDS.

- I AM CONSISTENTLY ETHICAL.

- I DO THE RIGHT THING ACCORDING TO WHAT I BELIEVE.

- I KNOW ETHICAL BEHAVIOR INVOLVES RESPECTING THE FREEDOM OF OTHERS.

- I KNOW THAT WE ALL HAVE DIFFERENT VIEWPOINTS ABOUT WHAT IS RIGHT AND WHAT IS WRONG.

- I OFTEN ASK, "WHY?" WHEN SOMEONE SAYS, I SHOULD DO SOMETHING.

- I TRUST THAT MY MIND CAN SET MY OWN MORAL COMPASS.

- I AM LEERY OF ANYONE WHO TELLS ME WHAT IS RIGHT FOR ME.

- I AM LEERY OF ANYONE WHO TELLS ME WHAT IS RIGHT FOR OTHERS.

47.
SHARE YOUR WISDOM

Happy people like to share their wisdom. Happy people like to make a difference by teaching others. We receive a large portion of happiness when we share some of our wisdom with another human being. When we can teach someone else even a little bit about what we have learned, not only do they benefit, but we also gain a great sense of satisfaction.

Those of us who are parents know how difficult it can be to share our wisdom, however. We can never force people to take our advice; all we can really do is offer suggestions or help them lay out their various options so they can figure out which way works best for them. We want to help our children, for example, avoid some of the pitfalls we went through in life, but if we try too hard, they rebel and go in the opposite direction. The bottom line, part of being human, is that we desire to make our own choices and decisions in life. No one really wants anyone else to tell them what to do, so we must always remain patient and remember that sharing wisdom has two parts: the sharing part and the receiving part. Sometimes we do a great job sharing but others aren't ready to receive the wisdom we have shared. We shouldn't beat ourselves up about that but know that we have done the best we could!

Sometimes people may ask our advice only because they want us to tell them what they wish to hear. If we live with personal integrity, we will find that impossible to do; we will be compelled to tell them only what we believe to be truthful. This will sometimes result in people becoming angry with us, but usually, they eventually apologize and thank us for giving a sincere opinion. It is not always easy to share our wisdom, but the rewards far outweigh the difficulties!

I like to imagine that
To make room for more wisdom,
I must give a little away each day.

CHAPTER 47
AFFIRMATIONS

- I FREELY GIVE AWAY KNOWLEDGE TO THOSE WHO ASK.

- I OFFER SUGGESTIONS, BUT I DON'T PROPOSE SOLUTIONS.

- I FEEL AWESOME WHEN I SHARE MY WISDOM.

- I AM CAREFUL NOT TO CONFUSE TEACHING WITH PREACHING.

- I KNOW THAT MESSAGES ARE RECEIVED WHEN LISTENERS ARE READY.

- I CAN INSPIRE OTHERS TO CREATE POSITIVE CHANGE BUT CANNOT FORCE THEM.

- I KNOW A HEARTFELT MESSAGE IS OFTEN WELL RECEIVED.

- I DISPLAY CARING WHILE I AM SHARING.

- I LIKE TO SHARE WHAT OTHERS HAVE TAUGHT ME.

- I ENJOY BEING A ROLE MODEL TO THOSE WHO NEED ONE.

48.

TRY NEW THINGS

If learning to laugh is the main ingredient to the fountain of youth, trying new things is a close second. A willingness to try new things creates a feeling of youthful happiness. We can become very unhappy by living lives that are too routine and mundane, and we may even lose our sense of childish wonder or the ambition to discover new things about ourselves and the world around us.

Taking chances in life is what trying new things is all about. Most of us are familiar with the phrase "nothing ventured, nothing gained." I don't think anyone can live without eventually encountering a few crossroads. It is always scary to take risks and to try new things, but our overall happiness levels depend on it.

I was inspired to write this chapter because of my mother, Marilyn, and my stepfather, Mel. My mother was seventy-two years old when her husband Archie passed away. Mel was eighty years old when his wife passed away. One day, they met in a grieving class for widows and widowers, and they quickly became great friends. Over a very short time, they fell in love and got married. I can't think of a better example of being open to trying new things, especially at their age. The happiness they have found by their willingness to love one another after suffering such tremendous losses is too incredible for words to describe. Let's just say they are both overjoyed that they took a chance and tried a new thing with each other! I am very proud of them both, and I will always look up to them as personal role models. They inspire me whenever I am unwilling to take a chance in life.

I took a chance
And found my wonderful wife.
She took a chance,
And we uncovered
A treasure chest of love.

CHAPTER 48
AFFIRMATIONS

- I AM OPEN TO NEW IDEAS.

- I TAKE EDUCATED RISKS.

- I LOVE TO TRAVEL TO DIFFERENT PLACES.

- I LOVE TO LEARN ABOUT VARIOUS CULTURES.

- I GO TO SEMINARS AND LECTURES.

- I LOVE TO READ BOOKS.

- I AM A WELL-ROUNDED PERSON.

- I HAVE MANY FUN AND INTERESTING HOBBIES.

- I EVALUATE RISKS AND THEN MAKE A MOVE.

- I ENJOY BEING A CREATIVE SPIRIT.

49.
MONEY MATTERS

We have all heard people say that money does not create happiness. I would venture to guess that anybody who says that doesn't have very much money. We all know people who have money and are still miserable and unhappy, and from this, some people falsely conclude that money cannot create happiness. We must remember, however, that these people would be miserable and unhappy no matter what their situation, so we shouldn't blame it on their wealth.

Now, I do agree that money cannot buy us happiness; happiness is an internal state that cannot be purchased. Money is an inanimate object that is utterly worthless when one is stranded on a desert island, but it is the most useful tool on Earth when one is *not* stranded on a desert island. Like it or not, money is society's form of trade. We cannot all be totally independent of each other. We all need services and products of others, and money allows us to purchase the things we need as well as the luxuries we desire.

Money can enhance our happiness in many ways. It can put food on the table, provide medical care, allow us to live in safe environments, and put clothing on our backs. It can also let us travel, it allow us to obtain higher educations, and allow us to buy products and services that make our lives more productive, efficient, and enjoyable.

Happy people realize that they can do many positive things with money. They are not greedy; they simply want to make better lives for themselves, and they appreciate and enjoy what money can do to enhance their lives as well as the lives of those around them.

Money cannot buy us happiness;
Money can enhance our happiness.
Money is not the root of all evil;
Greed and selfishness
Are the roots of all evil.

CHAPTER 49
AFFIRMATIONS

- I WILL EARN MY RICHES IN A WAY THAT BENEFITS OTHERS.

- I WILL REMAIN THE SAME PERSON WITH OR WITHOUT WEALTH.

- I CAN DO MANY GREAT THINGS WITH MONEY.

- I HAVE A POSITIVE ATTITUDE TOWARD WEALTH AND SUCCESS.

- I DESERVE TO BE AS RICH ANYONE ELSE.

- I KNOW ALL RICHES START WITH A SUCCESS-ORIENTED MIND FRAME.

- I LOVE TO BE GENEROUS WITH MY MONEY.

- I AM EXCITED ABOUT THE POSSIBILITIES THAT WEALTH OFFERS.

- I ENJOY HELPING OTHERS CREATE MORE WEALTH.

- I KNOW CONSTANT THOUGHTS OF WEALTH LEAD TO GREAT SUMS OF MONEY.

50.
SELF-RENEWAL

The day-to-day activities of living are strenuous and take their toll on us, sapping us of energy, so we all need to take time to regroup, refreshing and renewing our spirits, minds, and bodies. We can do this in various ways. A few include prayer, meditation, exercise, reading, hiking, fishing, camping, playing sports, dancing, playing instruments, listening to music, and painting.

Some people think renewal is something that we may do once a year, like a retreat or a seminar, but happy people take time out for self-renewal every day. Every day, we question who we are and where we are headed, deal with the difficult frustrations of human interaction and communication, and use our muscles to do work and to move our bodies around. It therefore only makes sense that we should take time to renew ourselves every day. Just as body builders must take time out to rest their muscles before they try to build them again, we must take time to renew ourselves. Self-renewal cannot be something we do as a last resort but is a necessary action that we must continuously take in order to survive at peak physical, mental, and spiritual levels.

If it is so important, why do we avoid taking time for self-renewal? We say things like "I am too busy," "I am too tired," "I don't have enough time," "I have too many other responsibilities," or my favorite, "I have more important priorities in my life." All these excuses amount to that we don't think we matter very much. We put ourselves on the bottom of the priority list. Happy people, however, realize that it is hard to be of good service to others if without being in proper physical, mental, and spiritual conditions themselves. If you can't seem to renew yourself for yourself, renew yourself for those who love you.

Every morning, remove yourself from,
The hustle and bustle of living.
Renew your spirit, mind, and body.
Find your inner peace.
Clear your negative thoughts.
Relax or exercise your body.
Prepare yourself
To meet the challenges of the day.

CHAPTER 50
AFFIRMATIONS

- I ENJOY SPENDING QUIET TIME ALONE EACH MORNING.

- I CONTEMPLATE, PRAY, OR MEDITATE BEFORE I SLEEP.

- I EXERCISE CONSISTENTLY TO KEEP MY BODY FIT AND TRIM.

- I FIND JOURNALING A RELAXING RETREAT FOR MY MIND.

- I OFTEN TREAT MYSELF TO NICE THINGS.

- I APPRECIATE THE BEAUTY AND SPLENDOR THAT THIS WORLD HAS TO OFFER.

- I ENJOY SPENDING TIME IN NATURE.

- I DEFINITELY PLAN FOR SOME "ME" TIME EACH WEEK.

- I REVIEW MY GOALS AND AFFIRMATIONS DAILY.

- I TAKE TIME TO STOP AND SMELL THE ROSES.

51.
STAND UP FOR YOURSELF

How long will a bully bully someone? As long as the bullied person allows it.

If we let people constantly push us around and manipulate us, we will be very unhappy. Although you can't really lose your self-esteem, you can definitely misplace it. Allowing others to pick on you without standing up to them will eventually do just that.

We all deserve respect; it is our inalienable right. We were all created equal. We do not have the right to physically or emotionally abuse other people, and they do not have the right to abuse us. Because we are born equal, we all have the right to stand up for ourselves when others think they have the right to take away our freedom of happiness.

Some people think that their status, position, or relation to us gives them full reign and authority to disrespect and abuse us, but they are wrong. No one is entitled to that power over anyone else. There are absolutely no exceptions to this! We may become intimidated by a boss, spouse, parent, teacher, coach, or friend, and we will continue to feel this way until we learn to become assertive enough to stand up for ourselves and to tell people how we truly feel. Most of us would easily stand up for someone else (even a total stranger) if they were being picked on, abused, or accused of something unjustly, so why won't we do this for ourselves?

We are worthy and deserving of respect, and like everyone else, we matter! Sometimes standing up for ourselves involves great risk, but I would rather protect my self-respect at all costs than live a life full of fear and trepidation. I must first care enough about myself before I can defend myself. Pride in oneself is not a sin when it is the same pride we feel for all living things. We should always value all forms of life, including our own.

We all put our pants on
One leg at a time;
Therefore, we all are worthy
Of the same amount of respect.
We do not have the right
To bully other people.
We all have the right
To stand up for ourselves.

CHAPTER 51
AFFIRMATIONS

- I AM MY GREATEST ALLY AND SUPPORTER.

- I STAND UP FOR WHAT I BELIEVE IS RIGHT.

- I AM ASSERTIVE BUT NOT OVERBEARING.

- I DEFEND MYSELF FROM ANY KIND OF ABUSE.

- I PROTECT MYSELF AS I WOULD ANY OF MY FRIENDS.

- I VALUE AND RESPECT MYSELF.

- I DO NOT ALLOW OTHERS TO BULLY ME.

- I HAVE THE COURAGE TO CONFRONT MY ENEMIES.

- I SET BOUNDARIES FOR WHAT I WILL TOLERATE FROM OTHERS.

- I AM A FEARLESS DEFENDER OF JUSTICE.

52.
CHOOSE YOUR REACTIONS

Sometimes we are unhappy because of the way we have automatically responded to a situation. If we had been able to choose our reaction, perhaps we would have felt differently. It's sad to say, but in some ways, we are exactly like trained monkeys; throughout our lives, we have been emotionally wired to automatically respond to certain stimuli. For example, if we were teased about our eyeglasses in school, we might as adults relive all those negative feelings every time we try on a pair. The only way to get over this reaction is to avoid eyeglasses or to reprogram our minds so we won't have negative reactions to glasses.

How can we learn to reprogram our minds to respond in more beneficial manners? The answer lies within our imaginations. If we want to learn how to control our reactions, we must rehearse different situations in our minds until we can clearly see ourselves responding in the manner we desire. If we attach positive imagery to eyeglasses and imagine ourselves wearing them and hearing people telling us how great we look, our subconscious minds will substitute this feeling for the negative feelings accompanying the old memory, and we will automatically respond in a positive way in the future.

We can use this technique to bring about change for just about any reaction, including anger, sadness, guilt, and fear, although the skill does take an enormous amount of dedication and practice to master. It is not something we can learn overnight. The effort is well worth it, however, because if we can learn to choose our reactions, we will be more in control of our moods, which will create much higher levels of happiness in our lives.

Rehearse your reactions.
Like a well-trained actor,
See your new behavior
In your mind's eye.
Practice it over and over again
Until your new response
Is accepted by your subconscious mind
And turned into reality.

CHAPTER 52
AFFIRMATIONS

- I CAN PROGRAM MY SUBCONSCIOUS MIND TO RESPOND AS I DESIRE.

- I KNOW MY IMAGINATION IS THE PATHWAY TO CHANGE.

- I AM NEVER TOO OLD TO RETRAIN MY AUTOMATIC REACTIONS.

- I REHEARSE THE WAY I WILL RESPOND.

- I AM IN CONTROL OF MY RESPONSES TO STIMULI.

- I PRACTICE IMAGINING POSITIVE OUTCOMES.

- I SEE AND FEEL MYSELF AS IF THE CHANGE HAS ALREADY HAPPENED.

- I CONSTANTLY FEED MYSELF WITH POSITIVE GOALS, THOUGHTS, AND AFFIRMATIONS.

- I AM ABLE TO MOVE ON FROM THE NEGATIVITY OF THE PAST.

- I CAN ALWAYS, ALWAYS, ALWAYS CREATE POSITIVE CHANGE!

CONCLUSION

When does happiness start? As soon as you desire it. Being happy is a lifelong process.

We will never find complete happiness, however; total happiness is a myth that does not exist. We are all equal in the fact that we are simply human beings trying to live our lives the best way we can. We are placed in various situations and circumstances, and we all encounter diverse obstacles and difficulties.

No one has the cure-all answer to happiness. If you hear anyone says they do, you might want to run away quickly! It is inevitably up to each of us to find out what makes us happy.

Because total happiness does not exist, seeking total happiness will only create more unhappiness. We can always seek a greater level of happiness, however; although we can never reach perfection, an infinite amount of self-improvement is available to assist us in experiencing more fulfilling lives.

Happiness is not made of one thing but is made up of various thoughts, values, and experiences. The sum of all these things creates our overall levels of happiness. I have tried my best in this book to share fifty-two suggestions for happiness that would be very difficult for anyone to disagree with, regardless of background or spiritual or political beliefs. I struggled to find common denominators to help all people live a happier life. It is my great hope and wish that I have succeeded in even the slightest way to provoke just one person to look within and discover and experience the joy and beauty of his or her own unique life. It is my deepest desire that we can all live large, love abundantly, and never stop learning. Let the journey begin!

Happiness is our right.
We don't have to earn it;
We just have to choose it.
We generate it within us;
We celebrate it amongst us;
We determine its meaning;
We grow it by believing.

Lightning Source UK Ltd.
Milton Keynes UK
UKOW01f0531040917
308541UK00010B/570/P